STEP-BY-STEP

CorelDRAW!
Versions 2.0/2.01
& 3.0

STEP-BY-STEP

CorelDRAW! Versions 2.0/2.01 & 3.0

John Campbell & Marion Pye

NEW TECH

Newtech
An imprint of Butterworth-Heinemann Ltd
Linacre House, Jordan Hill, Oxford OX2 8DP

PART OF REED INTERNATIONAL BOOKS

OXFORD LONDON BOSTON
MUNICH NEW DELHI SINGAPORE SYDNEY
TOKYO TORONTO WELLINGTON

First published 1992

British Library Cataloguing in Publication Data
A catalogue record for this book is available
from the British Library

ISBN 0 7506 0503 0

Printed and bound in Great Britain by
Biddles Ltd, Guildford and King's Lynn

Contents

About This Book

Part One: The Tool Box Drawing Tools

Part Two: Creating and Manipulating Text

Contents

Part Three: Shaping and Adjusting Objects

Part Four: Line and Fill Settings

Contents

Part Five: About Menus

Contents

Part Six: Quick Reference

Appendix A: Glossary

Index

About this book

Foreword

We have written this book to help you get off to a flying start with CorelDRAW!

When we first saw CorelDRAW! we were staggered by how powerful it was. It did so many things! It was like getting a crate of new drawing tools and the temptation was to try them all out at once. But while it may be fun to play with all the magical things you can do with CorelDRAW!, it is not the best way to learn how to use the system as a whole. You see, CorelDRAW! 2 (CD! from now on) is not just a new toolkit – it's a whole new workshop which will change the way you work and the things you can make. Getting CD! is like going to your local DIY superstore and ordering all the woodworking tools you're ever likely to need. You wouldn't dream of dumping them in a big heap on the workbench. You would take the time to sort them out so you know where to find just the tool you need, when you need it. That's what this book sets out to do. We have to assume that you have never seen CD! before and our job is to help you identify the tools in the crate, one-by-one and Step By Step.

That doesn't sound much like getting off to a flying start, so how is this book going to help? Well, if you think about your woodworking toolkit, you'll realise you use the same small selection of tools most of the time – screwdrivers, hammer, pliers, saw, set square, drill and the like – you may need the other tools, but some you will use only rarely. It is the same with CD! or any other toolkit. So, we shall concentrate on those CD! tools you will use most of the time. That way you will quickly get the feel of CD! and get a real understanding of how it ticks. Which, in turn, means you will be able to explore the more obscure features of CD! on your own and at your own speed.

Foreword

We have had to assume certain things about the computer system you are using. We have worked on the basis that our computer system is fairly typical. It is a single user 'PC 386' machine with a colour monitor, Microsoft Windows 3.0, a 40 megabyte (MB) hard disc, 4MB of memory, a mouse and a postscript printer.

The descriptions and illustrations in this book relate to our computer system, so, if you are using CD! on a network, you may experience the occasional small difference in how things work. For example, on our system we have elected not to use the Windows 'Print Manager', preferring to print directly to our printer. This suits our style of working, but it might not be so convenient for you.

We have also assumed that you will work along with the various procedures as we describe them, which might make you think that the illustrations are a bit superfluous, but there are good reasons for having them. In the first place you may not want to work along with us, you may prefer to just read the book, so it will help if you can see what goes on when you use the system. But, even if you do work along with the descriptions, and you get the real thing on your own computer, an occasional picture will help you check that you and we are looking at the same thing.

However you use the book, we hope it helps you get to grips quickly with CD!. Equally importantly, we hope you enjoy it. And if you do enjoy the book, you may like to think about a course on the subject. (See the end of this book for details of courses and other books in the series.)

John Campbell and **Marion Pye**

Tillington, Hereford 1992

How to use this book

The whole point of Step By Step books is to provide readers with detailed instructions on how to get results with their computer hardware and software. The books are a mix of background information and practical worked examples of typical procedures. As we work through an example we try to make the different types of information stand out from each other by using a standard set of layout conventions. The main narrative appears in body text which is the whole width of the page – like this paragraph.

When we work through a procedure, we break it down into steps and present each step in a numbered 'do-this' paragraph like this:

1   Turn on your computer.

2   Wait for it to go through its start-up procedure.

3   Start Windows and load Corel Draw.

When we want you to key-in something at the keyboard, the thing we want you to key-in normally appears **IN BOLD CAPITALS IN THIS TYPEFACE,** which is different from the normal one. In such cases it actually doesn't matter whether you key-in the thing in upper or lower case. When it does matter, we use upper and lower case in the instruction.

All the special keys on the keyboard, such as **RETURN, Alt, Ctrl, SHIFT, SPACEBAR, F1, F2,** etc. appear as they do here.

How to use this book

- When we are providing you with a list of items, we use bullet paragraphs like this one

- Any special notes, such as warnings or key points to remember, **are presented in this typeface.**

Note

Sometimes, when we are working through a lengthy procedure, it involves two or three distinct sets of activities. In such cases you will find that the 'do-this' numbering starts at 1 for each set of activities. (From time to time we add extra information, which may not be immediately obvious from the text or activity which precedes it. When we do so, it is in the form of a note paragraph like this one.)

When we ask you to **CLICK** on something, it means that we want you to move the mouse so the screen pointer is on an item and then click and release the **LEFT** hand mouse button just once. Sometimes we shall ask you to **CLICK** more than once and sometimes we shall be asking you to **DOUBLE CLICK** on an item. A 'double click' is two 'clicks' in quick succession. On other occasions we shall ask you to **CLICK AND HOLD** down the button and on yet others we shall ask you to **SHIFT CLICK** (hold down a shift key while you click the mouse button). All of these actions are with the left mouse button, but occasionally we shall ask you to **CLICK** the **RIGHT MOUSE BUTTON**. So if you are asked to do something with a mouse button, you can take it that we mean the left mouse button, unless we tell you otherwise.

PART ONE
The Tool Box
and its
Drawing Tools

Introduction

Corel DRAW! is much more than just a superlative drawing toolkit, in fact, its ability to handle and mould text is at least as impressive as its drawing capabilities. Here is a list of the sort of things you can do with Corel DRAW! versions 2 and 2.01.

- create drawings of objects of virtually any shape

- stretch, mirror, move, rotate and skew any image

- copy, cut and paste, duplicate and repeat images

- create special effects, like: 3D images, perspective images and 'blended' images

- create lines, curves, boxes and ellipses

- create text images of virtually any size and shape

- create image text and paragraph text

- use more than 150 typefaces from 75 families

- align text to a specific path

- use the huge symbols library

- specify different outline thicknesses and colours

- 'fill' shapes from a vast selection of colours and textures

- import and export images between different programs

- work with screen previews of the image you're creating

- save your work and print-out the end result.

Introduction

When you work with Corel DRAW! ('CD!' from now on) you use a range of 'tools' to create and modify objects (for the time being, think of text items as also being 'objects' – i.e. separate unique 'things' which can be modified in many ways.)

The CD! main work screen, looks like the illustration in Fig. 1-1 below. It has several components you need to know about. (Please start-up your CD! system now. If you don't know how to, see the sections on the File menu later in the book.) Centre screen, the box with a 'drop shadow', is a representation of the page of paper you are using. This is where you will create your image by working with the various CD! tools. You select the tools you want to use from the toolbox which you can see at the left-hand side of the screen.

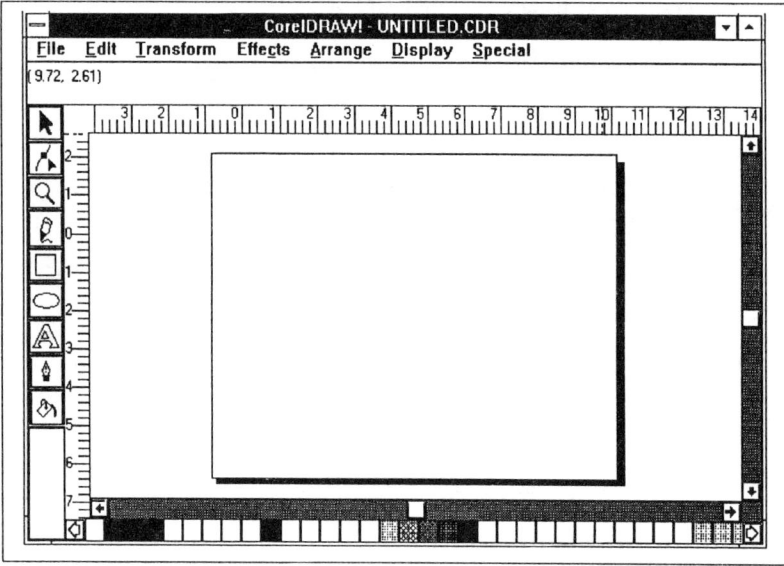

Figure 1-1 **The CD! work screen.**

Introduction

Across the top of the work screen you will see a selection of menus – seven in all – which enable you to manipulate objects, images and files in many different ways. We shall be examining each of the tools and menus in turn.

If you have just installed CD! for the first time, your screen will not look exactly the same as the one we show in Figure 1-1. It is a 'snapshot' of the screen on our system, which we have set up to suit our needs. So don't be surprised if this picture looks different from your screen. For a start we expect that yours will be in colour! And, if you look carefully at the toolbox, you will see we have had to doctor it slightly so it will reproduce clearly in black and white. It is also very difficult to represent CD!'s colour palette in black and white, as you can see at the bottom of the screen. You will also see that we have set up the rulers at the top and down the left hand side of the screen. But these differences are minor. Your screen will look very similar to ours, but not exactly the same.

But, just looking at the screen gives us no real idea of the power that lurks behind its neat image. So we want to begin our journey around CD! by getting a taster of the sort of things you can do with the CD! tools and menus. First, the tools.

There are only four drawing tools in the toolkit, see Figure 1-2. (To be pedantic, there are actually three drawing tools and a text tool, but who wants to be that small-minded!?) They appear in the middle, light section, of the diagram. We have shaded the upper and lower sections of the toolbox, to separate them from the drawing tools.

Introduction

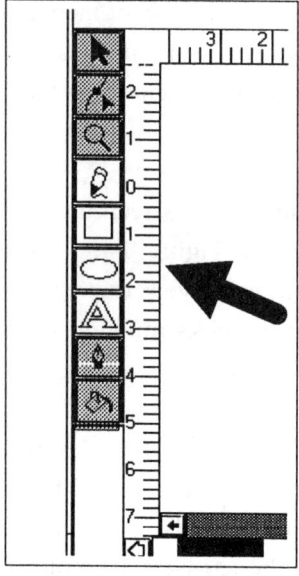

The upper shaded section contains three tools you will use while you are modifying and adjusting the objects you are creating. The lower shaded section enables you to specify different 'fills' and line thicknesses for the objects.

The actual drawing tools, the ones in the light coloured section, are:

- firstly, one for drawing lines and curves

- next, one for drawing rectangles and squares

- then one for drawing ellipses and circles and

- finally, one for generating text.

Figure 1-2
Corel DRAW! toolbox.

At first glance this may seem like a paltry selection of utensils, but read on! And try things out as we go along. We shall start with some basic exercises to get the feel of how things work. First, the drawing tools.

N.B. Throughout this book we shall assume that you have switched on your computer system, loaded Windows and then started CD!. In other words we shall be assuming that CD! is up and running. If you do not know how to get CD! running, see the section on the File menu at the rear of this book.

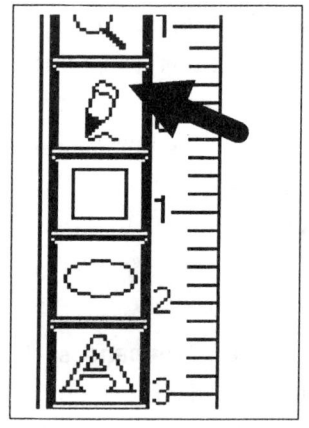

Fig. 1-3 **The Lines & curves icon.**

As with all the drawing tools, you select this tool by clicking once on the icon with the left hand mouse button. When you move your cursor away from the icon onto the main part of the screen, you'll see that the cursor is now in the shape of a cross, the lines of which do not quite meet in the middle – the 'Crosshair' pointer. If you have just started using CD! you will probably see the words **'Drawing In Freehand Mode'** appear in the status line – that is, in the blank space below the line of menus and above the work area of the screen. There are two drawing 'modes' with this tool: Freehand and Bézier. We shall look at freehand first. If your status line says, 'Drawing In Bézier Mode', then do this:

1 Move your screen pointer (with the mouse) so it settles on the **Special** menu (at the right hand end). Click once to make a flag menu drop down.

At the bottom of the flag menu you will see **'Preferences... ^J'** in black type – all the other options are in grey lettering. When you open up a flag menu, only the options in black lettering are available to you at that time. Most usually this is because you have not selected one of your objects for CD! to process. But, you do not have to select a particular object before setting your preferences, so this option is available now.

Drawing tools
Lines and Curves

2   Move your pointer down and click on the **Preferences... ^J** option. CD! will present you with a 'Dialog Box' (sic) which looks a bit complicated, so just ignore most of it for the time being and simply click on the long button at the lower left of the dialog box; the button marked '**Lines & Curves...**'. CD! will present you with another dialog box which looks like the one shown below in Figure 1-4.

3   Click on the little ('radio') button marked **Freehand** so it goes black – like the one in the illustration – then click on the **OK** buttons twice to get back to the work page.

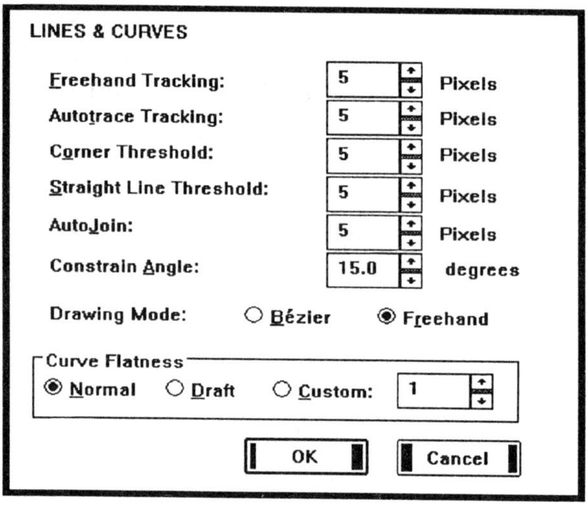

```
┌─────────────────────────────────────────────────────────────┐
│   ┌─────────────────────────────────────────────────────┐    │
│   │ LINES & CURVES                                       │    │
│   │                                                      │    │
│   │   Freehand Tracking:        ┌───┬─┐                  │    │
│   │                             │ 5 │▲│  Pixels          │    │
│   │   Autotrace Tracking:       │ 5 │▼│  Pixels          │    │
│   │   Corner Threshold:         │ 5 │ │  Pixels          │    │
│   │   Straight Line Threshold:  │ 5 │ │  Pixels          │    │
│   │   AutoJoin:                 │ 5 │ │  Pixels          │    │
│   │   Constrain Angle:          │15.0│ degrees            │    │
│   │                                                      │    │
│   │   Drawing Mode:    ○ Bézier    ● Freehand            │    │
│   │   ┌Curve Flatness─────────────────────┐             │    │
│   │   │ ● Normal  ○ Draft  ○ Custom: │ 1 │ │             │    │
│   │   └───────────────────────────────────┘             │    │
│   │                       │  OK  │   │ Cancel │          │    │
│   └─────────────────────────────────────────────────────┘    │
└─────────────────────────────────────────────────────────────┘
```

Figure 1-4   **The Lines and Curves preferences dialog box.**

Drawing tools
Lines and Curves

Now we are ready to start drawing lines and curves in Freehand Mode. Try these different things. (By the way, if you want to save the results of your experiments as we go along, see the sections on the File menu.)

1 The most straightforward way of getting results with the tool is to use the mouse like a pencil. Move your cursor (screen pointer) to a point near the top left hand corner. Now **CLICK AND HOLD** and move the screen pointer straight towards the bottom right hand corner. Stop near the middle of the page and then release the mouse button.

You will probably end up with a fairly wavering line. And you will notice that at various points along the line CD! has put little boxes. These boxes are called 'nodes' and they mark the points where your 'straight line' changes direction. So, in CD! terms, you haven't drawn a straight line at all. You have drawn a curve – i.e. a line with one or more changes of direction along its length. The fact that your line is a curve, and it has nodes on it, is important, as we shall be seeing. But that leaves us with the question, 'How do you draw a straight line?'

1 Move your screen pointer to a point close to the start of your first line (say, half an inch below it). Now **CLICK AND RELEASE** the left hand mouse button. Nothing seems to happen, but now move the screen pointer gently towards the centre of the page and you will see the screen pointer pull out an 'elastic' straight line from the point where you clicked.

Drawing tools
Lines and Curves

If you move your screen cursor around on the work-page you will see the elastic line track the cursor's movements.

2   Position the screen pointer near the centre of the page, with your straight line roughly parallel to your first line, and then **CLICK** to put the line in place.

This time you will see that your line has only two nodes, one at each end, which tells you that you have indeed drawn a straight line.

While you can see the nodes on any object you have drawn you can adjust the positioning and the 'look' of the object. For example you can delete it with the **'Delete'** key, or by holding down the **Alt** key and tapping the **BACKSPACE** key. **Alt+BACKSPACE** is actually the command to 'undo' the most recent action you have taken, so try this:

3   Tap the **Delete** key, to get rid of your straight line. Now hold down the **Alt** key and then tap the **BACKSPACE** key to undo the previous action and bring your line back again.

Notice that the nodes are still at either end of your line, so you can move either end of it. But you need another tool to move one node at a time. So, we'll stick with the drawing tool for the moment and we shall look at some other features that come into play when you are drawing straight lines with the click and release method.

Drawing tools
Lines and Curves

3 CLICK on the node at the end of your line nearest the centre of the page. Next, move the screen pointer down and to the right a little – so you draw out the elastic line an inch or two.

4 Now hold down the **'control'** key, probably marked **'Ctrl'**. Next, move the screen pointer toward the top of the page and watch your line.

You will see that, with the Ctrl key held down, your line moves in a series of jerks, rather than flowing smoothly with the pointer. This is because the Ctrl key 'constrains' the movement of a drawing tool to certain settings: Ctrl and the ellipse drawing tool constrains the tool to produce a perfect circle, Ctrl and the rectangle tool produces a perfect square.

Ctrl and the line drawing tool – in the click and release method – constrains the angle of your line to certain settings. Unless you have changed the setting, the angle of the line will change in fifteen degree increments. You can check this by seeing how many jumps the line makes as you move it from the horizontal to the vertical or vice-versa. You should find that it will make six jumps (6 times 15 degrees = 90 degrees), but a far easier way is to look in the status line at the top of the screen. You will see that CD! keeps track of the angle of the line you are drawing. You should see it change in increments of 15 degrees.

By the way, you can let go of the Ctrl key now, because we want to look at something else.

Drawing tools
Lines and Curves

5 Move the screen pointer so it draws out the line to a position near the top right hand of your page and then CLICK twice!

6 Now move the screen pointer and you will see the elastic line move from the node.

So, clicking twice is the quick and easy way to place the end of one line and the start of the next in exactly the same position.

Note

If you think back to the first straight line you drew, you will remember that you clicked to mark the beginning of the line and then clicked again to mark the end. You then had to position the screen pointer exactly over, or at least very close to, the node at the end of the line. This enabled you to join the second line to the first. Had you missed the node, then the lines would not have been joined. We shall see the significance of this in a moment.

Figure 1-5, opposite, is a repeat of the illustration in Figure 1-4. The last time we saw it we concentrated on the little round 'radio' buttons to check we were drawing in freehand mode. This time, notice the last two items in the main part of the box: **'Constrain Angle'** and **'AutoJoin'**. Here you can see the settings we have been talking about. And this is where you change them. (Assuming you want to, of course!)

The 'AutoJoin' setting tells you how close one line has to be to another before they will join. In this case, provided one line gets within five pixels (screen picture elements) of another, the two lines will join automatically when you place the line you are drawing.

7 Stretch your latest line away from the top right hand corner to the start of the first straight line you drew. We want you to join the end of this third line to the start of the first so we can create a triangle. When you have the screen pointer located over the very first node, **CLICK** to join the lines and make a closed triangle.

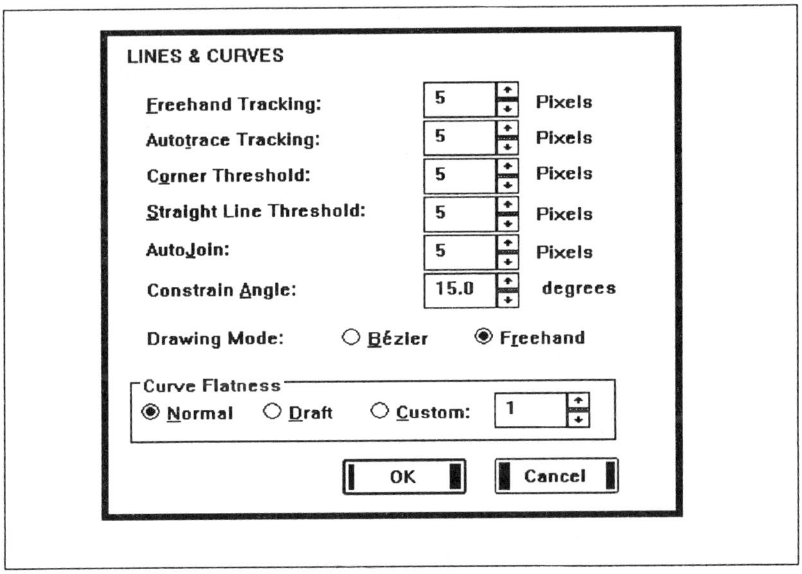

LINES & CURVES

Freehand Tracking: 5 Pixels
Autotrace Tracking: 5 Pixels
Corner Threshold: 5 Pixels
Straight Line Threshold: 5 Pixels
AutoJoin: 5 Pixels
Constrain Angle: 15.0 degrees
Drawing Mode: ○ Bézier ● Freehand
Curve Flatness: ● Normal ○ Draft ○ Custom: 1

OK Cancel

Figure 1-5 **The Lines and Curves settings on our system.**

Introducing
The Pick tool

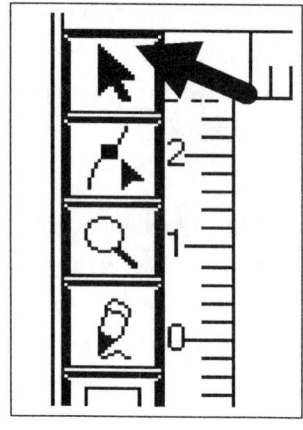

Fig. 1-6
The Pick tool icon.

In the next section we want to look at drawing lines and curves with CD!'s Bézier Mode, but before we go ahead with that it would make sense to start with a clean worksheet. This involves getting rid of the drawing you have done and that in turn involves a few new concepts.

Getting rid of the work you have done is really just a matter of using the Delete key, except it is often better to do something else first. If you tap Delete now (while you are using a drawing tool), you will simply get rid of the object which has its nodes showing. But you may not want to do that – you may want to get rid of something you prepared earlier, or you may want to get rid of more than one of the objects. In our case we want to get rid of the triangle and the freehand line we drew. If that is what we want CD! to do, we have to tell it.

So how do we tell CD! what to delete? Well, we have to start by 'picking' out the objects we want to delete. Now that probably sounds a bit daft at the moment because there are only two very simple objects on the screen, but as you get into producing more complicated images, which contain many different objects, then you begin to see the sense of this approach.

Introducing
The Pick tool

You can pick out the objects you want to select for deletion (or any other form of processing) in a few ways and we shall try them all. We have to start by selecting the 'Pick' tool – and there are two ways of doing this:

1 Watch the screen and tap the **SPACEBAR**.

Notice that the crosshair screen pointer changes to a black arrow and eight little black boxes appear on the screen. The black boxes tell you something has been selected, or 'picked', for processing (in this case, the triangle). Notice what the status area is saying.

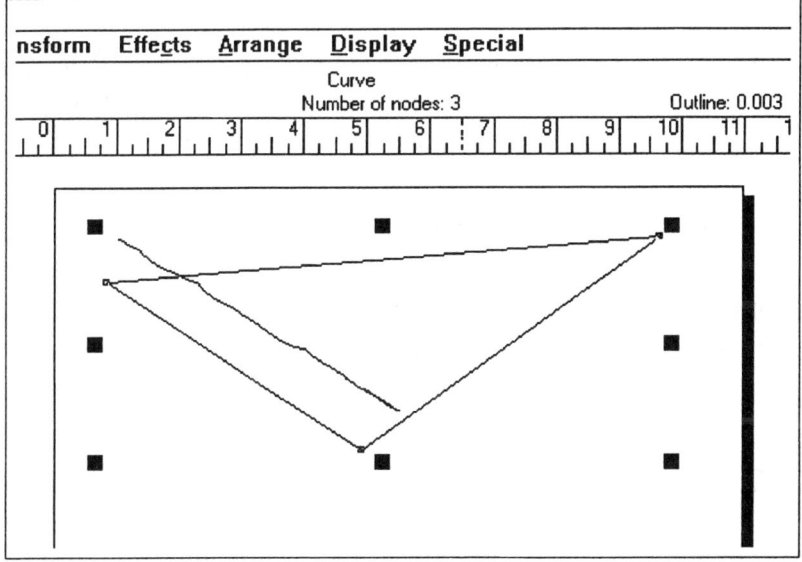

Figure 1-7   **One item 'picked' for processing.**

Introducing
The Pick tool

In this instance the thing you were drawing is selected (because the nodes were still showing on the object when you tapped the spacebar). But in the illustration it looks as if everything has been selected. It hasn't, but we <u>can</u> select everything if we want to.

2   Tap the **SPACEBAR** again, and you go back to the drawing tool you were using.

So, tapping the spacebar 'toggles' between the drawing tool you are using and the Pick tool. The second way to activate the Pick tool is to select it, like any other tool, from the toolbox.

3   Move your screen pointer to the topmost button in the toolbox – the one which has on it a black arrow pointing up and left – and **CLICK** once.

You will see the button darken and, when you move the screen pointer back onto the work area, you will see that it is now in the shape of a black arrow. The little black boxes should also appear again – don't worry if they don't, because we want you to clear them now in any case.

1   Move the screen pointer onto a blank part of your page and **CLICK** once.

The little black boxes will disappear.

Introducing
The Pick tool

If you want to select both objects you have drawn, you can do it in two ways. The first is a method known as 'Marquee Select'. (Before you ask, we don't know precisely why it's called that!)

1 Move your screen pointer so it is above and to the left (or below and to the right) of the objects you want to select for processing. Then **CLICK AND HOLD** and **DRAG** the cursor to the opposite corner of an imaginary rectangle.

As you move the screen pointer, you will see a blue elastic rectangle grow to enclose the objects. It will look something like this.

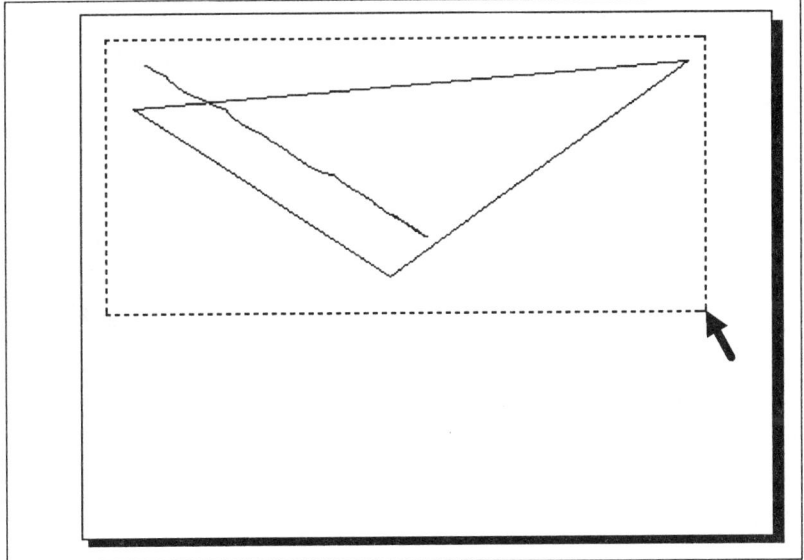

Figure 1-8   **Pick - 'Marquee' select.**

Introducing
The Pick tool

2   When the objects you want to select are completely enclosed, release the mouse button. You will see the little black boxes reappear as before. But this time all the objects are selected for processing.

You can confirm that by looking at the status area and by doing this:

1   Tap the **Delete** key and both objects should disappear. Now tap **Alt+BACKSPACE** to undo your last action and to bring back your objects again. Then **CLICK** on a blank part of the page to 'de-select' the objects.

We can now have a look at the second method of selecting objects for processing.

1   Move the screen pointer so the point of the arrow is on the freehand line you drew first. **CLICK** and release the mouse button and you will see another set of little black boxes appear. This set is different from the ones you've had before.

Look carefully at the status area of the screen. Right in the middle, CD! is telling you what has been selected – a curve, with a certain number of nodes – as well as some other information we can examine later.

So that is how you select a single object for processing. To select more than one:

2   Hold down either of the SHIFT keys and then CLICK on the outline of the triangle you drew.

You will see the little black boxes rearrange themselves. Once again, the status area tells you what has been selected. It should now say, **'2 objects selected'**.

1   And now, since both objects are selected, and since the whole purpose of this little excursion has been to look at how to clear the page, tap the **Delete** key.

Note

There is yet another way to select all the objects on the page, via the **Edit** menu, but we shall look at that when we examine how the various menus work.

Drawing tools
Lines & curves tool
Bézier mode - lines

Let's start by selecting the Bézier drawing mode.

1 Hold down the **Ctrl** key and then tap the letter **J**. (The shorthand for key combination is Ctrl+J, or Ctrl-J, or ^J.)

CD! uses 'control codes', like Ctrl+J extensively and we shall be looking at them at the relevant times.

2 When you get the PREFERENCES menu, click on the **Lines & curves...** button and when you get the LINES & CURVES dialog box click on the little radio button, labelled **Bézier**.

3 Then click twice on the **OK** buttons to get back to the work screen.

We can draw straight lines and curves in Bézier mode and we shall start by looking at lines.

1 Begin by clicking on the line drawing tool (just in case). Now move your cross shaped screen pointer to a position close to the left hand edge of your work page and about half-way down. Keep your mouse still and **CLICK** once, to put a small black node on the page.

2   Next move the screen pointer to a point close to the edge of the top of the page, about half-way across and **CLICK** again.

CD! does two things here. Firstly it places a second node on the page and secondly it draws a straight line between the two nodes on the page.

3   Now move your screen pointer half-way down the right hand side of the work page and **CLICK** once more. And then move to the middle of the bottom edge of the page and **CLICK**.

So far you have drawn three sides of a rectangle, which by itself is no big deal. But notice the key point here, that in Bézier mode CD! continues linking the nodes until you tell it to stop. (This is true for all drawing tools and we'll show you how you stop it in a moment.) This means you can draw intricate straight line patterns very easily. Like this:

4   Move the screen pointer to a position half-way along the first line you drew and **CLICK**. Then move to a position half-way along the second line you drew and **CLICK**, then half-way along the third line you drew and **CLICK** ... and continue the process as far as you can to create a spiral pattern like the one in Figure 1-9.

Remember that when you have finished the pattern, the drawing tool will still be active and ready to continue the pattern even further.

Drawing tools
Lines & curves tool
Bézier mode - lines

If you place the pointer anywhere else on the page now and CLICK again CD! will link another line from the last node in your spiral, to this new one. Now this is very annoying and a bit messy if you want to create two separate drawings – joined up writing is one thing, but joined up drawings is quite another! Fortunately it is very easy to separate your drawings.

1 Just tap the **SPACEBAR** twice. You will see the little black 'selection' boxes appear and then disappear again.

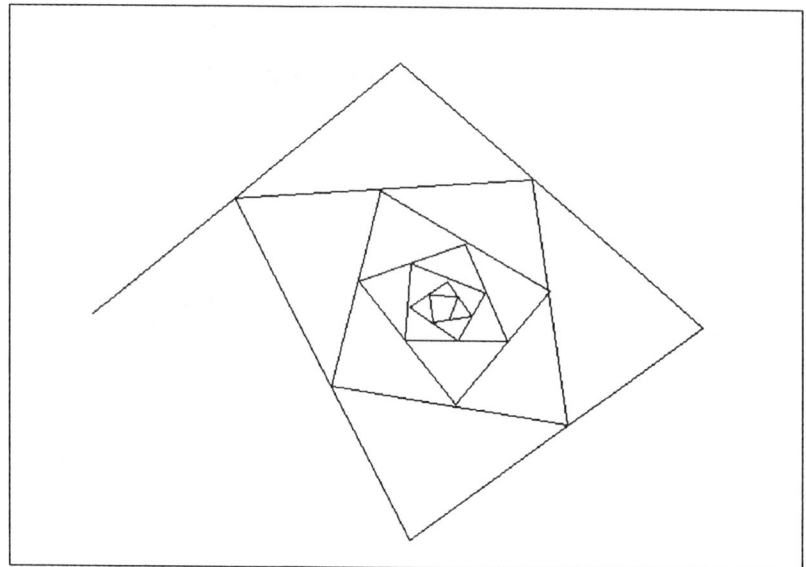

Fig. 1-9 **A straight line spiral drawn in Bézier mode.**

Drawing tools
Lines & curves tool
Bézier mode - lines

So tapping the SPACEBAR twice, 'toggles' the selection tool on and then 're-toggles' the Lines & curves drawing tool. In other words, the way to 'de-activate' a drawing tool temporarily is to select some other tool. This does not work for all the tools. If you select the magnifying glass, or the pen nib, or the paint pot tool, the drawing tool stays active. So the surest way to de-activate the drawing tool is to select the 'Pick' tool ... and the easiest way to do that is to tap the SPACEBAR, once to select the Pick tool and once more to reselect the drawing tool you were using.

Let us clear the page again.

1 Tap the **SPACEBAR** just once, and then tap the **Delete** key, then tap the **SPACEBAR** again to reselect the drawing tool.

If you hold down the Ctrl key while you are using the line and curve drawing tool in Bézier mode, CD! will constrain the straight lines to paths which follow angles that are exact multiples of 15 degrees from the previous node. Try this.

1 Move the screen pointer so it is near the left hand side of the page. Hold down the **Ctrl** key and **CLICK** once to place a node on the page. Keep the **Ctrl** key held down and move the pointer to the right and slightly down. Watch the screen as you **CLICK** once more to place the second node.

Drawing tools
Lines & curves tool
Bézier mode - lines

You should see CD! draw the line exactly horizontal (i.e. above the screen pointer's position), putting the second node precisely the same distance down the page as the first one.

2   Tap the **Delete** key to clear the page again.

The lines we have seen so far have been 'open objects'. That is, they do not completely enclose an area of the page. Objects such as rectangles, ellipses and triangles are 'closed' objects. So what? we hear you saying. But the concept of open and closed objects is important in CD! graphics because you can 'fill' closed objects with different colours, textures and effects and you can bound them with lines of different thicknesses and patterns. With open objects you can specify only that their lines should be of a certain thickness or pattern.

But notice, just now we listed three types of closed object: 'rectangles, ellipses and triangles' and we could also have mentioned other multi-sided objects, such as hexagons, septagons, octagons – in fact any number of gons. CD! provides you with two, only two, tools to draw closed objects, rectangles and ellipses. So how do you draw the other closed objects?

We examine a quick way next, but first let us see how you can get an instant preview of the work you are doing, because the work page alone can be a bit misleading sometimes.

Drawing tools
Lines & curves tool
Bézier mode - lines

1 Hold down either of the **SHIFT** keys and tap the **F9** key. CD! splits the screen for you. On the left is your work page, on the right is a representation of how the finished page will look.

Note

The SHIFT+F9 combination works at any time, not just in Bézier drawing mode.

The split screen preview will enable you to see a number of points about open objects and closed objects and about lines and fills. We shall start by creating the most simple closed object, a triangle. And we shall see along the way that just because an object looks closed, is no guarantee that it is.

1 Start by clicking to place your first node in the top half of the left side of the page. Then move across to the right hand side of the page, at about the same height, and place the second node. Now move the pointer down near the bottom of the page, and a bit left, and place the third node. Now move the pointer up so it is about half way along the first line you drew and place it exactly on the line. Then **CLICK** to join the third node to the first line.

The Line and Fill tools

If you have done it correctly, the page preview should show what looks like a closed triangle on the right of the page.

2   Now move the screen pointer to the pen nib, '**Line**' tool and **CLICK** once to select it.

This causes CD! to offer you a 'Fly-out' menu of 'Line Attributes' options, see Fig 1-10. This menu works just like the tool box, in that you make selections by clicking on the option (or 'attribute') you want to assign to the line(s) of the object you are working on. The top line of the fly-out menu allows you to choose a thickness for the line and the lower line allows you to choose a shade of grey.

1   Move your screen pointer onto the top line of the fly-out menu, onto the third icon from the right – notice that the screen pointer is still in the shape of a cross, because the drawing tool is still active. Keep an eye on the preview page and **CLICK** once to select the line thickness.

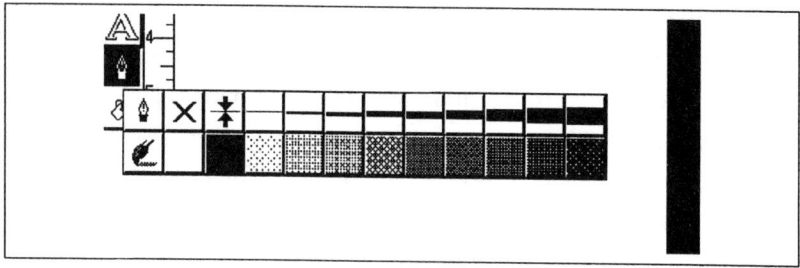

Fig. 1-10   **The 'Line Attributes' fly-out menu.**

The Line and Fill tools

Notice also, near the top right hand corner of your screen there is an indicator box with an 'X' in it. This box tells you two things: Firstly, the X tells you that your object has no fill, and secondly, the boundary of the box tells you the thickness of the line you have selected.

The Fill tool, just below the Line Attributes tool, also has a fly-out menu of options which you can choose for your objects. We shall deal with this menu (and the Line attributes menu) in detail later on in the book. But you can also select a fill for closed objects simply by selecting one from the palette at the very bottom of your screen. So:

1   **CLICK** the left mouse button on a fairly bright colour on the palette. (On our screen we have a nice bright red near the left hand end of the palette, so we shall click on that one.)

Note

You can scroll the colour palette by clicking on the arrows at either end, so we cannot be sure how yours is set at the moment – for all we know, you may have already tried scrolling the palette.

Nothing has changed on the preview. And neither has the indicator box at the top right of your screen, but you have drawn what looks like a closed object, so you might think that you should be able to fill the object. But look just to the left of the indicator box, in the CD! status area and you will see that the object you are drawing is an open path, even though it looks closed. But now do this:

The Line and Fill tools

1 Move your screen pointer toward the left hand end of the very first line you drew and then down towards the bottom of the page a short way ... and CLICK.

2 Now move the screen pointer up to the very first node you drew when we started this little exercise.

3 When your screen pointer is exactly on the first node, keep an eye on the preview screen and CLICK.

If you clicked accurately on the first node, you should see things change this time. Your double triangle should fill with the colour you chose and the indicator box should echo the result.

Why should the indicator box duplicate what you can already see on screen? Well, you may have already noticed that working with the split screen preview slows things down noticeably, yet the drawing we have created is very simple object. When you are working with more complex objects and images, you will probably want to work as quickly as possible, so you will probably choose to create your images with just the work page on screen. The indicator box is there to give you a quick impression of how the particular object you are drawing will look. But remember that a complex image will be made up of several separate objects. When you need a more detailed view of the whole image – as opposed to just the object you are drawing – that is when you need to get a page preview. And you can do this in two ways. For the first, as you have seen, you tap SHIFT+F9, the second method we shall examine next.

The Line and Fill tools

Let us start by cancelling the split screen preview, (we don't have to, but we want to show you how the work page looks now):

1 Tap **SHIFT+F9** to toggle the split screen preview off again.

Notice the indicator box in the top right hand corner of the screen.

2 Now tap **F9** on its own to get your preview of how the page will look when it is printed on a colour printer.

When you have the full page preview on screen, none of CD!'s tools work, so all you can do is look. To get back to the work page (or the split screen preview if that was where you came from):

3 Tap the **SPACEBAR**.

Note

In fact you can tap any of the keys that do something on their own. For example you can use the Tab key or the Caps Lock, but not a SHIFT key, Alt, or Ctrl, all of which are designed to alter the function of other keys, rather than produce direct end results of their own. And we suggest you get into the habit of tapping the SPACEBAR simply because it is bigger than all the other keys ... and is, therefore, easier to find in the middle marches of the night the deadline expires.

The Line and Fill tools

So the object you have drawn has lines and a fill. More precisely, it actually has only one line and a fill. In fact, to be really pedantic, as far as CD! is concerned, it has one curve and a fill; as you will see if you look in the middle of the top line of the status area. So all these lines we have been drawing have not been lines at all!

As far as we laymen/women are concerned, a straight line is the shortest distance between two points. For CD! it is the shortest path between two nodes. Likewise, what we would call a curve, is a line which does <u>not</u> take the shortest route from one point (or node) to the next. So these 'node' things are obviously important to CD! In fact they are very important. You use them to shape and adjust the things you draw. We shall be coming back to nodes many times during this book and we shall see, for example, that there are different kinds of nodes, and that you can add, delete and transform them, but that is for later on. For the time being just let us accept that the straight lines you have drawn are in fact curves, and as such are capable of being edited in a variety of ways.

But, whether we are talking about a straight line or a curve, we see it as a line on the computer screen or the paper. At the moment your object has a black line of a certain thickness. You have seen how to change the thickness of the line, but how do you change the colour?

1 As it is some time since you drew and filled the object, just check that the indicator box is still showing the fill colour and the line thickness (and colour, i.e. black). If it isn't, select the **Pick tool** and click on the outline of your object.

The Line and Fill tools

2 Move your screen pointer down to the colour palette at the bottom of the screen and find a bright colour which will contrast well with the fill colour you chose. (We have a bright green which will do for us.)

3 Get ready to click the **RIGHT mouse button** (not the left this time)!

4 Move the screen pointer onto your chosen colour for the line and **CLICK** the **RIGHT mouse button** once.

5 Look at the indicator box to get an impression of the effect of the change. Then tap **F9** to get a full page preview.

Our picture looks pretty vile, like a logo for a 'heavy metal' band, so let us quickly put it right again.

6 Tap the **SPACEBAR, CLICK** on the pen nib icon in the tool box and then **CLICK** on the solid black option – third from the left in the lower row of options.

The indicator box will show you that the line is now black again.

So... you can change the characteristics of your lines (and the fills for your closed objects) either through the tool box, or by clicking on the colour palette – (with the **LEFT** mouse button for fills) with the **RIGHT** mouse button for lines.

Drawing tools
Lines & curves tool
Bézier mode - curves

Just to get things straight, in this section and on most other occasions when we talk about 'curves', we mean any line which does not follow a straight path between two nodes.

You have already had a go at drawing a freehand curve. You probably ended up with a very ragged looking squiggly line which was nothing like the perfectly smooth curving line you drew with the mouse. Well in Bézier mode you can create very smooth flowing curves. With a bit of practice you can create precisely the shape you want. But it does take a bit of experimentation to get things exactly right. So what we recommend is that you work through the examples on the following pages, which will highlight the basic factors involved, and then try several experiments of your own.

Let us begin by clearing our work page again.

1   If you have worked through the previous pages, then all you should have to do is to tap the **Delete** key. If you have been doodling while you have been waiting for us, select all the objects first, by selecting the **Pick tool** and then drawing a **'marquee'** (see page 23) around them, before tapping **Delete**.

You should still have the Line and curves drawing tool selected and you should still be in Bézier mode.

Drawing tools
Lines & curves tool
Bézier mode - curves

Drawing curves in Bézier mode, like drawing straight lines, is really a matter of joining up points. The difference between a curved line and a straight one is that the curve follows a certain 'trajectory'. That trajectory is determined by three main elements:

- The angle at which the line leaves the start point

- the 'height' it attains

- and the distance to the finish point.

It follows then that you need some way of controlling all these elements. The distance to the finish point is easy enough to determine; you just put your second node where you want the curve to end. But how do you determine the other two? Lets look at each one in turn.

First determining the 'height' of the trajectory.

1   Move your screen pointer so it is quite near to the left hand side of your work page and as close as you can get to half-way down the page. Then **CLICK AND HOLD DOWN** the mouse button.

2   Now move your mouse so the screen pointer moves vertically upwards on the page. As you move you will see two 'handles' grow outwards from the start node. Keep moving until the upper handle reaches the top of the work page. Then **RELEASE** the mouse button.

Drawing tools
Lines & curves tool
Bézier mode - curves

3   Now move your screen pointer to the right hand side of the page, so it is about the same distance down the page as the start node. **CLICK** once to place the second node of our curve and then tap the **SPACEBAR** twice so we can draw a second separate curve.

Notice the shape of the curve CD! has drawn for you. It starts with a steep angle from where you placed the first node, reaches a certain height and then swoops down smoothly to where the second node is.

Now we shall draw a second curve and we shall keep the start angle, and the distance between the two nodes, the same (as nearly as we can). All that will be different about curve 2 is the height.

1   Move the pointer to a position directly above where you placed the first node for curve 1 and about half way between the start of curve 1 and the top of the page. **CLICK AND HOLD** and 'grow' the handles so the upper one reaches the top of the page, as before, then **RELEASE** the mouse button.

This time the handles will be about half as long as for curve 1.

2   Next, as before, move the screen pointer to the right hand side of the page, directly opposite the start of curve 2, and above the end of curve 1, then **CLICK** to get the second curve.

Drawing tools
Lines & curves tool
Bézier mode - curves

As you examine the two curves you have drawn, remember that they are the same, except for the height. Which tells us that the length of the control handles at the start node control the height of the curve. In Figure 1-11 below you will see a series of curves drawn with this method. notice that they are all of about the same height and they are 'cusped' – i.e. adjacent curves meet at a point where there is a node.

Now we can move on to looking at how you determine the start angle of the curve, and here too we shall draw a path made up of cusped shaped curves.

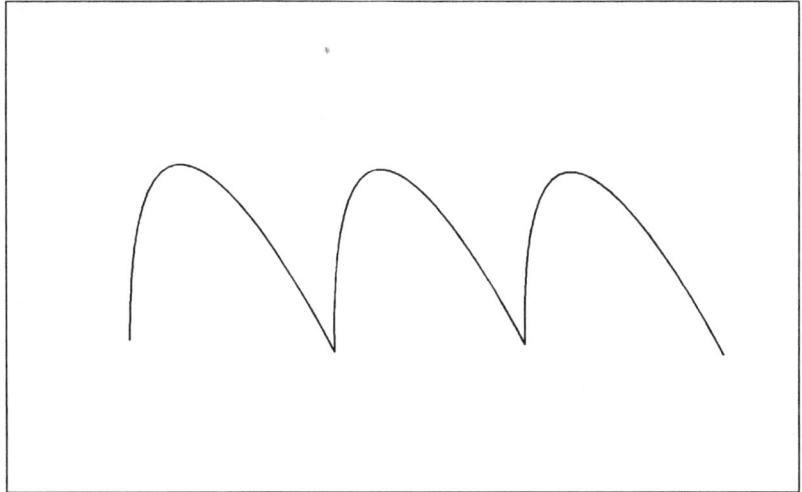

Fig. 1-11   **'Cusped' shape curve drawn in Bézier mode (nodes at points, omitted for clarity).**

Drawing tools
Lines & curves tool
Bézier mode - curves

Once again, begin by clearing the page. We shall leave you to do it on your own this time.

1   Place the screen pointer as nearly as you can to the centre of the top edge of the page. **CLICK AND HOLD** and pull out the control handle horizontally to the **RIGHT**. When you reach the edge of the page, **RELEASE** the mouse button.

2   Put the screen pointer about an inch above the bottom of the page and directly below the first node. **CLICK** to draw the curve, then tap the **SPACEBAR** twice, ready to start a second curve.

3   Place the screen pointer immediately below, but clear of the start node of the first curve. **CLICK AND HOLD** and draw out the control handle to the **LEFT**. When you reach the edge of the paper (i.e. when this control handle is about the same length as the first one you did, just now), **RELEASE** the click.

So we know that both curves in this test will be of about the same 'height' (because the control handles are of about the same length). But the start angle will be different – one will be +90 degrees from the vertical and the other will be -90 degrees from the vertical, because we pulled the control handles in different directions. If we now make the shared vertical 'baseline' of the curves the same, then we should end up with curves that are identical except for the start angle.

Drawing tools
Lines & curves tool
Bézier mode - curves

Remember, one curve goes right and the other will go left, but the height and the length will be roughly the same for both curves.

4   Move the screen pointer so it is immediately below, but clear of, the second node of curve 1 and **CLICK** to draw the second curve. Then tap the **SPACEBAR** twice to finish the curve.

In summary then, it is the length and angle of the control handle which determines the basic shape of the curve. Or to be a bit more precise, it controls, what you might call the 'leading edge', or the front end of the curve. But you can also control the trailing edge of the curve. Try this:

1   Clear the work page and then reselect the **Lines & Curves** tool. Near the middle of the left hand side of the page, **CLICK AND HOLD** the mouse button and draw out the control handle vertically to the top of the page, then **RELEASE**.

2   Place the screen pointer near the centre of the page, on about the same level as your start node, then – **and this is different from before** – **CLICK AND HOLD** the mouse button and pull out another control handle vertically to the bottom of the page.

Watch the screen and **keep the mouse button held down for a moment!**

Drawing tools
Lines & curves tool
Bézier mode - curves

3   Keep an eye on your curve and try swivelling the control handle slowly from side to side.

Note

Try shortening and lengthening the control handle and notice what happens. You will see that you have complete control over the shape – the height and angle – of the curve. Take some time to experiment.

4   When you have seen enough, **RELEASE** the click, move the screen pointer near to the right hand side of the page – again at about the same level as the first node – then, **CLICK AND HOLD** and draw out the control handle to the top of the page again.

5   **RELEASE** the click and finally tap the **SPACEBAR** twice to finish the curve.

You should end up with a smooth curve like the one in Figure 1-12. Contrast this with the 'cusped' shaped curve in Figure 1-11 (repeated at the top of the next page). In particular notice where the nodes are in Figure 1-12. And make allowances for the fact that both these illustrations are 'screen snapshots', which make the lines look more jagged than they will on the page. The key point of both illustrations is the general shape of the curve.

Drawing tools
Lines & curves tool
Bézier mode - curves

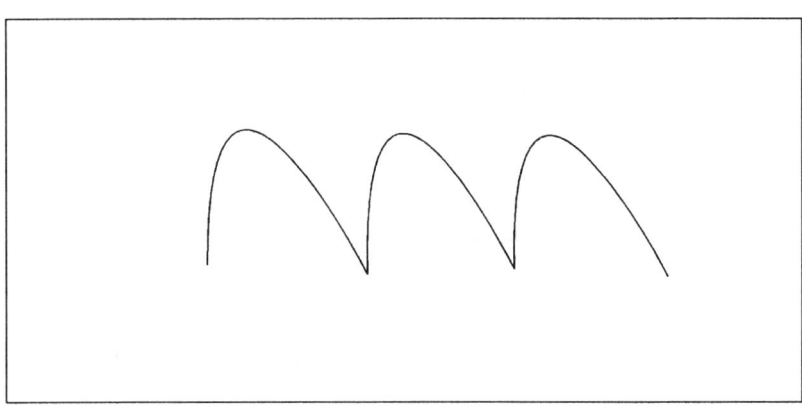

Fig. 1-11 (repeated)   **'Cusped' shape curve
drawn in Bézier mode – (nodes at points, omitted).**

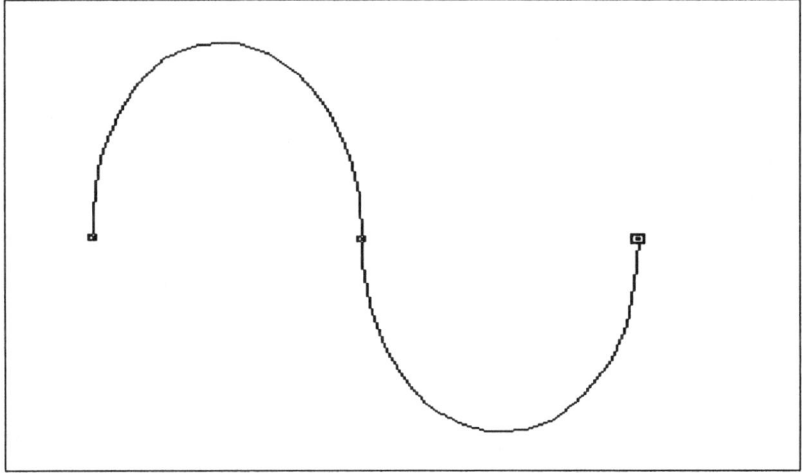

Fig. 1-12   **Smooth curve drawn in Bézier mode.**

Drawing tools
Lines & curves tool
Bézier mode - curves

Figures 1-11 and 1-12 on the previous page, illustrate the difference between a smooth curve and a cusped curve.

Broadly speaking, in a path made up of cusps, adjacent curves enter and leave a node on the same side. In a path which is a smooth curve, one part of the path enters one side of a node and the next part leaves the node from another.

CD! creates different kinds of nodes, depending on the precise shape of the curve you draw. In fact it can create a 'line' node and three kinds of 'curve' nodes: cusp, smooth, or symmetrical. As we shall be seeing, the different types of node give you different ways of controlling the shape of the path you are drawing.

We have been talking rather loosely when we said that the curve in Figure 1-12 is a 'smooth' curve – it seems to imply that the nodes on the line are 'smooth' nodes. Certainly the general shape of the path is smooth, but, in this case, CD! has put two different kinds of node on the line. At each end there is a cusp node and the one in the middle is a symmetrical node (because the curves on either side of the node are the same).

The fact that there are different kinds of nodes is not important for the moment, but it will become so when we look in more detail at nodes. We make the point now, merely to avoid confusion later in the book.

Drawing tools
Rectangles

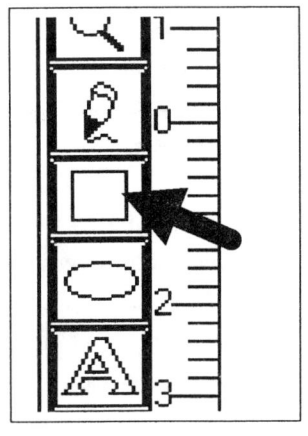

Fig. 1-13
The Rectangle icon.

Now you have seen how to use one drawing tool, you will find that they are all very similar. We are sure that you can use the rectangle tool by yourself, but, just for the record:

- There is no click and release method for drawing rectangles – use click, hold and drag to create your rectangle

- If you want to 'constrain' the rectangle tool to draw squares, hold down the Ctrl key as you did for the Lines and Curves tool

- Notice where CD! puts nodes.

Having made those points, we can try using the tool.

1 Make sure that your work page is clear.

2 As usual when you want to create a shape on the page, start by selecting the drawing tool you want. Move the screen pointer to the tool box and CLICK on the **Rectangles tool**.

3 Move your pointer back onto the work page. Notice the screen pointer is in the crosshair shape for this tool, as it is for all of them.

Drawing tools
Rectangles

4 Place the pointer somewhere near the top left corner of the page. **CLICK AND HOLD** and then move the pointer to the right and downwards to drag out an elastic rectangle. When the rectangle just about fills the page **RELEASE** the click.

With this method you draw out a rectangle from its top left corner, but you can draw it out from any corner. It all depends on which direction you move the mouse after you have clicked and held. So the 'click' (of the CLICK AND HOLD) fixes one corner of your rectangle and the 'drag' pulls out the opposite corner. When you 'release' the click, that action fixes the opposite corner.

If there is a shortcoming of this method, it is that you cannot be absolutely certain of the shape of the rectangle you produce. Most monitors give a distorted impression, so it is difficult, for example, to produce an exact square. Luckily CD! has a solution.

1 Move the screen pointer crosshairs so they sit just inside the top right hand corner of the rectangle you have just drawn. Now hold down the **Ctrl** key and then **CLICK AND HOLD** and move the crosshairs down and to the left, then **RELEASE** the mouse button **before** you release the Ctrl key.

CD! constrains the rectangle to be a perfect square, though, you probably won't be able to tell that from the screen. But you will see the square grow in steps, rather than smoothly as before.

So far you have seen how to fix the corners of a rectangle and make the rectangle or square grow from one corner. But what happens if you want to centre your rectangle on a specific point?

1   Move the crosshairs onto one corner of the square you have just drawn – say, the top left corner. Hold down one of the **SHIFT** keys, then **CLICK AND HOLD**. Now move the mouse down and right and watch the rectangle grow from the centre, rather than from a corner. Keep the **mouse button** and the **SHIFT** key held down.

2   If you can manage it, now hold down the **Ctrl** key as well (perhaps with your thumb). Move the screen pointer and you will now see a perfect square growing from the centre. Once more, **RELEASE** the mouse button before you release the other keys.

You will see on the square you have just drawn that CD! puts a node at each corner. You may have also noticed this when you drew the other rectangles. Like the nodes on the lines and curves you have drawn, these are special points which allow you to control the shape of the object you have drawn. When we look at the Ellipse drawing tool you will see it creates nodes as well. But the nodes on lines and curves, on rectangles and on ellipses all behave slightly differently and they give you different results. For the time being it is enough to realise that all your objects have nodes on them somewhere.

Drawing tools
Rectangles - Fills and Lines

Rectangles are closed objects, which means that you can fill them with colour and pattern (as well as define certain thicknesses and patterns for their outlines). So we shall do this next.

1 Start by tapping the **SPACEBAR** to activate the **Pick tool**. The tap **SHIFT+F9** to get the split screen preview.

2 Working on the work page at the left of the screen, **CLICK** on the outline of the big rectangle you drew first. Then **CLICK** on a colour in the palette at the bottom of the screen. Repeat the process for the other rectangles/squares you drew, filling each one with a different colour.

3 Then, **CLICK AND HOLD,** above and to the left of all the objects on the work page ... and draw out the blue dotted outline to 'marquee select' all the objects. Make sure you fully enclose all the objects on the work page, then **RELEASE** the click.

4 Select the pen nib **'Outlines'** tool and when you get the fly-out menu, **CLICK** on the third icon from the right in the top row.

So now all your rectangles have different fills, which you specified individually, and they all have the same thick line around them, because you selected all the objects before adjusting the line thickness. Remember you can change the colour of the outlines by clicking on the palette with the right hand mouse button.

Drawing tools
Ellipses

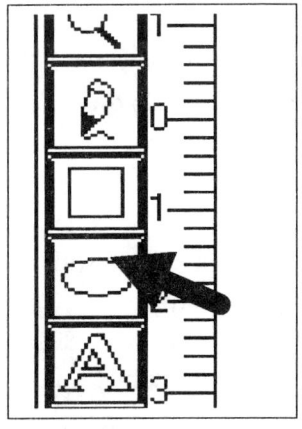

Fig. 1-14
The Ellipse icon.

The Ellipse drawing tool is as easy to use as the Rectangle tool. In fact, it works in exactly the same way. Here too, we expect that you can use it by yourself, but, again just for the record:

- There is no click and release method for drawing ellipses – use click, hold and drag to create them

- If you want to 'constrain' the Ellipse tool to draw perfect circles, hold down the Ctrl key as you did for the Lines & Curves tool and the Rectangles tool

Having made those points, we can try using this tool now.

1 Start by making sure you have a clear work page. If you have worked straight through the previous page of this book, simply tap the **Delete** key. Then give yourself some more room to work, by cancelling the split screen preview. (Tap SHIFT+F9.)

2 CLICK on the **Ellipses** drawing tool.

Notice the screen pointer is in the crosshair shape again. This tells you that you have a drawing tool selected.

Drawing tools
Ellipses

3 Place the pointer somewhere near the top left corner of the page. **CLICK AND HOLD** and then move the pointer to the right and downwards to drag out an ellipse. When it almost fills the page, **RELEASE** the click.

What you have done here is draw out an imaginary rectangle (containing the ellipse) from its top left corner. But, as we saw with the rectangle tool proper, you can draw it out from any corner. It all depends on which direction you move the mouse after you have clicked and held. So, here too, the 'click' (of the **CLICK AND HOLD**) fixes one corner of your imaginary rectangle and the 'drag' pulls out the opposite corner. You fix the opposite corner by releasing the click.

Notice that your ellipse has a single node.

1 Move the crosshairs back to the top left hand corner of the work page. This time imagine a rectangle which extends only half-way across the page and from the top edge to the bottom edge. **CLICK AND HOLD** ... and drag out the imaginary rectangle to create an ellipse of a different shape from the first one. **RELEASE** the **CLICK** to fix the ellipse.

2 Next, move the crosshairs to the extreme right hand edge of the ellipse you have just drawn. Hold down a **SHIFT** key and the **Ctrl** key.

3 **CLICK AND HOLD** ... and move the crosshairs slowly down and to the right, to draw out a perfect circle centred (approximately) on the work page. Finally, **RELEASE** the mouse button and **then** the **SHIFT** key and the **Ctrl** key. Tap the **SPACEBAR**. Your screen should now look something like Figure 1-15.

While you are using the Ellipse tool, it will help you if you imagine yourself drawing a rectangle which contains an ellipse; particularly if you remember that Ctrl constrains the rectangle to a perfect square ... and SHIFT causes it to grow from the centre rather than a corner. You will be able to place the ellipses much more accurately on the page.

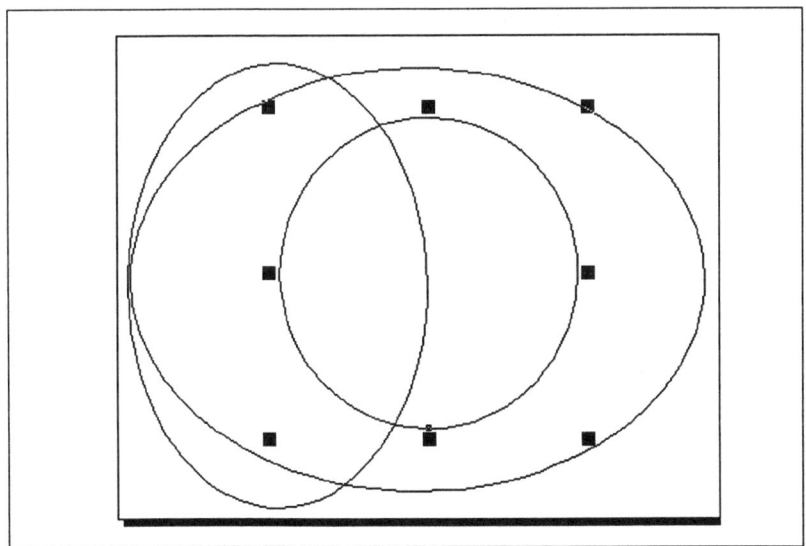

Fig. 1-15 **Various ellipses produced with CD!.**
Note the outline of an imaginary square around the middle circle.

Drawing tools
Ellipses - Fills and Lines

Ellipses and circles are also closed objects. This means that they too can be filled with colour and have their lines modified. In fact all closed objects behave just like rectangles in this respect, so we can repeat the exercise we did a few pages back.

1   The Pick tool should already be activated, so tap **SHIFT+F9** to get the split screen preview.

2   Working on the work page at the left of the screen, **CLICK** on the outline of the big ellipse you drew first. Then **CLICK** on a colour in the palette at the bottom of the screen. Repeat the process for the other ellipses/circles you drew, filling each one with a different colour.

3   Then, **CLICK AND HOLD**, above and to the left of all the objects on the work page ... and draw out the blue dotted outline to 'marquee select' all the objects. Make sure you fully enclose all the objects on the work page, then **RELEASE** the click.

4   Select the pen nib Outlines tool and when you get the fly-out menu, **CLICK** on the second icon from the right in the top row. (Remember you can change the colour of the outlines by clicking on the palette with the right hand mouse button.)

5   Tap **Delete** to clear the work page and we can go on to look at something else which relates to all the objects you draw.

Sizing objects

1 Tap the **SPACEBAR** to get the Ellipse drawing tool back. Move the crosshairs into the very middle of the work page, then hold down a **SHIFT** key and draw an ellipse. Leave plenty of white space around it.

2 Tap the **SPACEBAR** again to toggle back to the **Pick tool**.

You will see the little black squares on screen which tells you that you have 'selected' the ellipse for processing in some way. So far in this book we have simply referred to the little black squares as 'little black squares' without explaining what they are for. In fact they are 'Sizing handles' and the best way to define what that means is to get you to use them.

We shall do that in a moment, but first, notice that there is one handle at each corner of a rectangle which surrounds the object – it is always a rectangle, even if you have selected a line or a curve for processing. That accounts for four of the eight handles. The other four are in the middle of the sides of the rectangle. So you have two types of handle and they do different jobs.

1 Move the arrow shaped screen pointer onto one of the corner handles, say, the bottom right hand one. You will see the pointer change to a cross shape when you are over the handle. **CLICK AND HOLD**.

If you miss the handle, you will de-select the object. Just CLICK on the outline of the ellipse to re-select it and try again.

Sizing objects

As soon as you move the mouse you will see it change to four arrows pointing North-west, North-east, South-west and South-east. At the same time you will see a blue 'elastic' boundary box appear around the object. If you move the screen pointer absolutely horizontally or vertically on the page, nothing else happens, but if you move it diagonally in any of the four directions, you will see the blue elastic box grow or shrink in size. But you will notice that the aspect ratio (the proportion of height to width) of the box remains the same. Notice that the corner opposite the one you have 'grabbed' stays fixed in position.

2 RELEASE the click to fix the object at the new size. Then move to one of the side handles, say, the one in the middle of the right hand side, and **CLICK AND HOLD**.

This time when you move the screen pointer it changes to two arrows, one pointing East and the other pointing West. The same would happen if you clicked on the left side handle. Had you clicked on the top or bottom side handle the two arrows would point North and South. As before, the arrows tell you the direction of 'stretch' the handle governs. This time notice that as you stretch or shrink the box, the side opposite the handle stays fixed and the height remains the same.

3 RELEASE the click to fix the object to its new shape.

Sizing objects

The SHIFT and Ctrl keys also have a function when you are sizing objects. Their effect is analogous to the way they change the behaviour of the drawing tools, as we can see now:

1 Begin by grabbing the **bottom right corner handle** of your object and shrinking the elastic box until it is really very small on screen.

When you release the click you will still be able to see the sizing handles quite clearly.

2 Hold down the **Ctrl** key and then grab the bottom right handle again. Watch the screen and start to stretch the elastic box diagonally down and to the right.

At first nothing will seem to happen, then you will see the blue box growing in jerks – each jerk being a step, proportional to the size of the object before you started stretching it.

3 RELEASE the **Ctrl** key and shrink the object again. Make it a little bigger than you made it just now. Then RELEASE the click.

4 Hold **Ctrl** down again and this time grab the **top side handle** and start dragging slowly **downwards**.

Sizing objects

At first nothing will happen, but when you reach the lower edge of the existing ellipse you will see the blue box flip down below the object. If you were to release the click at this stage, you would have created a mirror image of the original picture – mirrored top to bottom, but not left to right.

5   Keep pulling gently downwards and you will see the blue box stretch in steps again. Notice the width of the box stays constant. When the blue elastic box reaches somewhere near the bottom of the page **RELEASE** the click to reveal a tall thin ellipse.

Note

You may think this is too obvious to say, but we shall say it anyway; when you change the shape of the blue elastic box, the object changes shape to fill the box exactly.

So that is how the Ctrl key modifies the effects of the sizing handles, and you may like to experiment a bit further, but leave your experiments until after we have seen how the SHIFT keys modify the their operation.

1   Hold down a **SHIFT** key and grab the **right side handle**. Drag the screen pointer to the right and watch what happens to the blue box. You will see it grow by the same amount either side of the centre line.

2 Keep the SHIFT key held down, but RELEASE the click and then grab the **bottom right corner handle**. Watch the screen and move the screen pointer diagonally toward and away from the centre of the ellipse.

You will see the blue box grow and shrink about the centre point of the object.

3 Now hold down the **Ctrl** key as well. Move the pointer in and out again and watch as the blue box grows and shrinks in steps as before, but still around the centre point of the object.

4 Keep SHIFT and **Ctrl** held down, but RELEASE the click. Now try the same experiment with one of the side handles, say the **top** one.

5 When you have seen enough, RELEASE all the buttons and keys and let the blood rush back into your fingers.

N.B. You can 'flip' images simply by shrinking the object past its 'minimum point'.

Try some experiments now on your own to get the feel of the sizing controls.

Drawing tools
Moving an object

An image you create with CD! will normally be made up of more than one object. For example, the screen dump of the masterpiece in Figure 1-17, 'Desert Sunset', is made up of five separate closed objects: two rectangles, two triangles and a circle. You can see the principal components in Figure 1-16.

You will have to take our word for it, but Figure 1-17 was produced simply by rearranging the objects in Figure 1-16. We had to tweak the fills a bit, but that is not the key point here. The fact is, we were able to move the various objects on the page to get them in the positions you can see in Figure 1-17. So how did we do it?

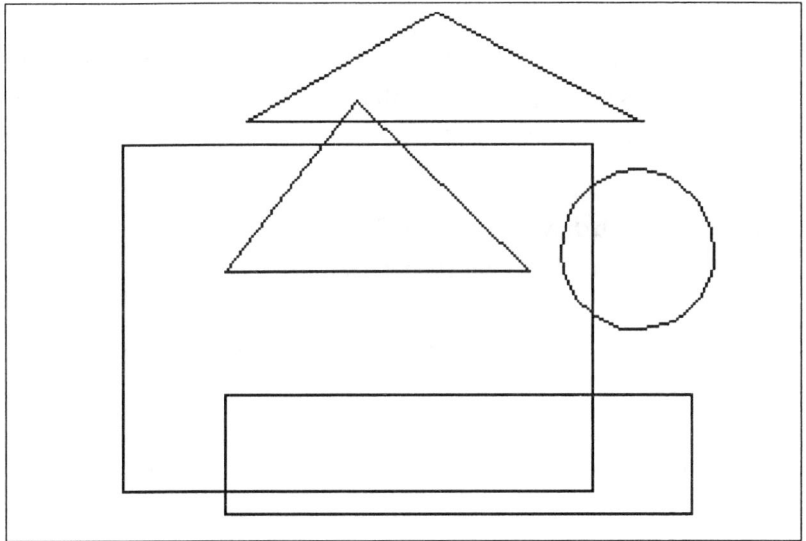

Fig. 1-16 **Components of the 'Desert Sunset' masterpiece.**

Moving objects is actually very easy – it has to be, because, no matter how skilled you are, and no matter how powerful the software you are using – it is difficult to place objects with absolute accuracy while you are drawing them. So the more sensible way of working is to create the objects in approximately the right position and then use CD!'s facilities to get them in exactly the right place.

To demonstrate this, we shall have to ask you to create a couple of objects which we can move about.

1 Start by making sure you have a blank work page.

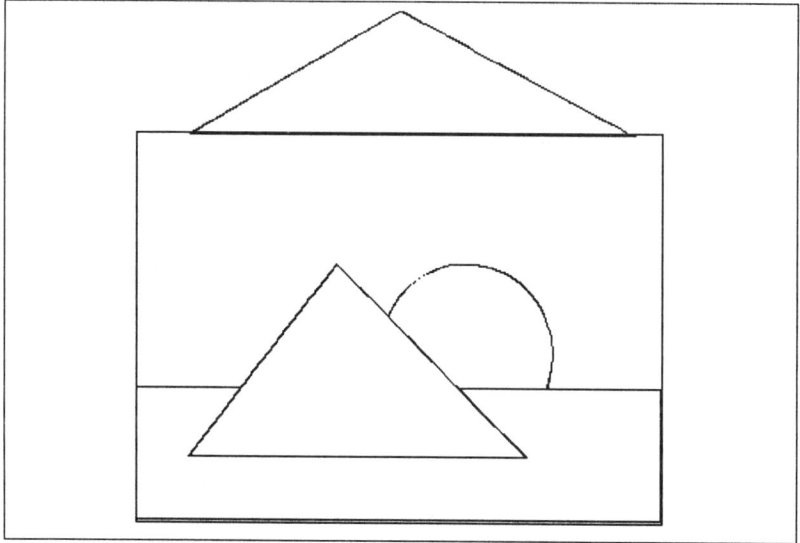

Fig. 1-17 **'Desert Sunset' by Mozart, age 7.**

Drawing tools
Moving an object

2   If your screen is set up for the split screen preview, cancel it with **SHIFT+F9**.

We want you to draw a perfect circle and a triangle in different places on the page. Then we want you to move the circle so it balances on the point of the triangle. A simple enough exercise, but one which will let you see the various options open to you.

1   In the top right hand corner of the work page, draw out a **perfect circle**. As you draw it, keep an eye on the top line of the **status area** where CD! will tell you the height and width of the 'ellipse' you are drawing. Make the circle about **2 inches (50mm)** high and wide.

2   Select the **Lines & curves tool**. You should still be in Bézier mode (the top line of the status area will tell you if you are or not). If you are not in Bézier mode, select it as you did before, by tapping **Ctrl+J**, opening up the **Lines & Curves** dialog box and then clicking on the **Bézier** radio button.

3   Move the crosshair pointer so it is near, but clear of the bottom of the page, about one third of the way across from the left side. **CLICK** once to place a node, then move the crosshairs to a position about two thirds of the way across the page from the left and at about the same height as the first node. Hold down the **Ctrl** key and **CLICK** again.

Moving an object

4   Next, move the crosshairs so they are in the very centre of the page and **CLICK** to position the node for the apex of the triangle. And finally, **CLICK** again on the first node to complete the triangle. Tap the **SPACEBAR** to activate the **Pick tool**.

So we now have our two objects in different places on the screen and we are ready to bring them together. The easiest way to do that is to move the circle down and across to the point of the triangle, so that is what we shall do. But before we can process an object in any way we have to select it with the Pick tool. As your screen is now, you will see that it is the triangle which is selected, so:

1   Move the arrow shaped pointer onto the outline of the circle and **CLICK** to select it ('pick it') for processing. You will see the familiar sizing handles appear.

2   Place the pointer onto the outline of the circle again, but this time **CLICK AND HOLD.** The sizing handles will disappear. Now start moving the screen pointer down and to the left and you will see a blue dashed square move with the pointer.

The blue square is a representation of the object you are moving.

3   Move the blue square so the middle of the bottom edge sits on top of the triangle, then **RELEASE** the click.

Moving an object

The sizing handles reappear, making it virtually impossible to tell if you have positioned the circle accurately. You can get around this in a variety of ways, for example you could work with the split screen preview on, or you could get a full page preview, or you could simply de-select the object to get rid of the sizing handles. Let us take the last one first. You can de-select an object by:

- selecting another object

- selecting another tool

- clicking on a blank part of the work page.

The problem is, if you deselect the object and you find that you still need to adjust its position slightly, then you have to re-select the object before you can make the change. This may not sound like much of a problem but it can become irritating if you are in full creative flow.

The problem with the split screen preview is two-fold; firstly, you have to work on a smaller image (although we shall be looking at ways of 'zooming-in' to work on fine detail) and secondly, if you are working on a complex image it may take some time to refresh the amended picture.

You have the same problem when you opt for a full page preview, but, the difference is, you only have to select the full page preview when you want it; it is not being refreshed continuously. All-in-all the full page preview seems to us to be a good compromise, so let's look at a little tweak which might speed things up for you.

1 Tap **Ctrl+J** to get to the PREFERENCES **dialog box.** CLICK on the button labelled **Mouse.** CD! will present you with a range of functions you can assign to the right hand mouse button. The fourth one down is **Full screen preview...** CLICK on the little **radio button** beside that setting and then CLICK on the OK buttons to get back to your work page.

2 Now CLICK the RIGHT **mouse button** to get the full page preview and see how accurately you have placed the circle.

3 Take a careful look to see if you need to make further adjustments and if you do, CLICK the RIGHT **mouse button** again (or tap the SPACEBAR) to go back to the work page.

This little task is actually harder than it seems at first and if you are like us, you may have to make several slight adjustments before you get it absolutely right. So alternate between the work page and the full page preview (using the right mouse button) until you are satisfied that the circle really does balance on the point of the triangle. When you get it right we can move on to look at something else.

Note

You can still use the right mouse button to change the colour of outlines, even though you have given this extra function to it.

Moving multiple objects

Now that we have so carefully positioned the circle on the point of the triangle, the page looks bottom heavy. It would be nice to move the drawing more to the middle of the page. But, of course we don't want to go all through the rigmarole of moving the triangle and then positioning the circle again. We need a way of moving all the elements of our image in one go.

1   The circle should still be selected for processing, so **HOLD DOWN** a **SHIFT** key and then **CLICK** on the outline of the triangle.

You will see the sizing handles re-arrange themselves to enclose the whole image. This means that you can move the whole image as one unit, like this:

2   **CLICK AND HOLD** anywhere on the outline of the triangle or the circle, and then move the blue rectangle gently upwards until it looks as if it is in the right position and then **RELEASE** the click. Check the result and adjust the position if you need to.

When you are happy with the result we can move on to doing some more experiments, using the techniques we have examined in the last few sections.

1   Hold down a **SHIFT** key and grab the **bottom right corner handle**. Shrink the picture until it is about half its current size.

You may have to move the shrunken picture a little to get it back in the middle of the page.

1   Hold down the **Ctrl** key, then grab the **top side handle**. Move the screen pointer downwards gently until the blue rectangle flips over. Then **RELEASE** the **mouse button** before you release the **Ctrl** key.

2   Next, **CLICK** on a blank part of the page to de-select the objects. Then **CLICK** on the outline of the triangle to select it. Now move down to the palette at the bottom of the screen and click on a colour.

3   **CLICK** on the outline of the circle and select another colour from the palette.

4   Now move the crosshairs back onto the work page and **CLICK** the **RIGHT mouse button** to get a full screen preview.

It seems right and proper that we end these sections on the drawing tools with a picture of a medal ... or, if you prefer, a multi-coloured exclamation mark!

PART TWO
Creating and Manipulating Text

Working with text: Some background

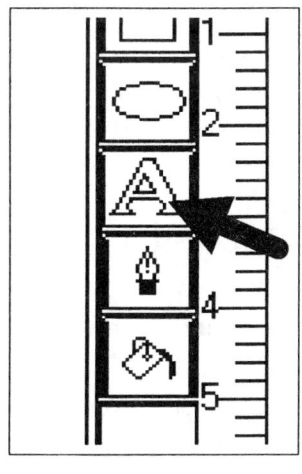

Fig. 2-1
The Text icon.

It is fairly safe to say that when you are working with text, you will want to use it for different reasons. For example, let us say that you are producing a small leaflet for a product, or a service, or even a jumble sale at the village hall. You will want the text on the leaflet to do different jobs.

You will want eye catching headlines and you will want good old stolid information. Ideally you will want one lot of text to be short and sharp and very impressive, while the other is neat and clean and more extensive.

For the headline you may want to change the shape, angle, typeface, colour and size of individual words, or even individual characters within a word. You may want the text to look three dimensional, or seem to recede into the distance, or change subtly from one style to another as it progresses. In short, you will want it to grab people's attention.

As far as the solid information is concerned, once you have designed the basic layout, you will want it to be clear and uncluttered, but most importantly, you will want it to be easily identified for what it is and you will want it to be easily read. In short, you want it to hold people's attention once the headline has grabbed it.

Working with text:
Some background

So you really need two kinds of text – one in which you can manipulate individual word shapes and the other which you can treat as a complete block at a time. CD! enables you to create both types of text. In CD! terminology, the first type of text is known as 'String' text and the second is known as 'Paragraph' text.

The way you create the actual text which appears on the page is the same for both types. What is quite different, though, is the way you place the text and what you can do to the text once you have created it.

With string text you place the words directly on the page. You begin by selecting the text icon and then moving the crosshair screen pointer to the position where you want the words to start. You then click on the page to tell CD!, firstly that you want string text and secondly, where you want it put. With paragraph text you begin, as before, by clicking on the text icon, but then you move the crosshairs onto the screen, click and hold and drag out a 'box' to hold the text. This action tells CD! you want paragraph text and the size and position of the box tells it where you want the text to appear.

The next step, with both string and paragraph text, is to create the text itself; and it is the same procedure for both types ... except, you can generate up to 250 characters of string text, or up to 4000 characters of paragraph text. If we take it that an 'average' word is about 5.5 characters then that equates to about 45 words of string text and just under 730 words of paragraph text. (N.B. According to our word count programme, there are 300 words on this page.)

Working with text: Creating new text

When you create string text, on the page, you can directly manipulate the shape and size of the text itself, just like any other closed object you create; a rectangle, or an ellipse, or a triangle, or a polygon. When you create paragraph text you cannot directly manipulate the shape or the size of the words, but you can manipulate the boundary box. When you change the size or shape of the text boundary the text may rearrange itself within the box, but it retains its size and alignment.

If we get some text on the page, things will become a lot clearer. We shall create a small section of both kinds of text; first, 'String text'.

1 Clear your work page and then CLICK on the **Text icon** in the toolbox. Move the crosshairs to a position close to the top left hand corner of the work page and CLICK once.

CD! will display a dialog box which contains a lot of items. Don't worry about all the items for a moment, we shall examine them in detail shortly. For now, just notice that you have a bar cursor flashing in the top left hand corner of the screen.

2 Key in these words: **Grand jumble SALE!** and then CLICK on the **OK** button and watch the screen.

Notice that each character you have keyed in has a control node at the bottom left corner.

Working with text:
Creating new text

You have generated some string text, now for paragraph text.

1   Move the pointer so it is just below, but clear of the 'G' in 'Grand'. Hold down the **Ctrl** constrain key, then **CLICK AND HOLD** and drag out the shape of an elastic blue dashed square. When it is as wide as the text, **RELEASE** the mouse button.

After a short pause you will get the same text dialog box on screen again. (You might notice a slight difference but we shall look at that soon.) Once again:

2   Key-in these words (don't worry about carriage returns, CD! looks after that for you): **2 o'clock at the church hall on the last Saturday in May. Old ladies with shopping trollies will not be allowed in.** (If you hit a wrong key by mistake, tap the BACKSPACE key to delete it, and then key it in again properly, CD! will make space for it.) Then tap **RETURN** ... and key-in: **Don't miss it!** and, finally, **CLICK** on the **OK** button.

Note

Notice that when you tapped the RETURN key it did not cause CD! to implement your instructions. You had to CLICK on the OK button. This enables you to key-in more than one paragraph of text at a time and it allows you to skip lines if you want to.

Working with text: Creating new text

So you have created both kinds of text, but we would be surprised if you were impressed by what you see on your screen. How can you get more pleasing results in future? As usual with CD!, there are several ways:

- You can specify a range of settings for the text, as you generate it

- You can change the colour and texture of the text

- You can change the position of the text

- You can change the shape of the text.

We shall look at all of these, starting with the first one in the list.

Specifying settings while generating text

You do this through the dialog box you have already seen. You will remember it is almost the same dialog box for string and paragraph text. Figure 2-2 shows the main part of the dialog box, but you may like to select it on your screen so you can experiment with the changes as we go along. Here's how:

1   CLICK AND HOLD on the work page, draw out a rectangle and RELEASE the click to get the dialog box for paragraph text.

You have already used the big box at the top of the screen, but we need to say a little more about it.

Working with text: Creating new text

The text entry box gives you access to a basic word processor; not a full-blown word processor, but one which has the essential controls.

Basic editing controls

- **RETURN,** as you know, ends a paragraph of text and enables you to put in blank lines

- **BACKSPACE,** deletes the character to the left of the bar cursor – it 'deletes to the left'

- **Delete,** gets rid of the character under the bar cursor – it 'deletes to the right'.

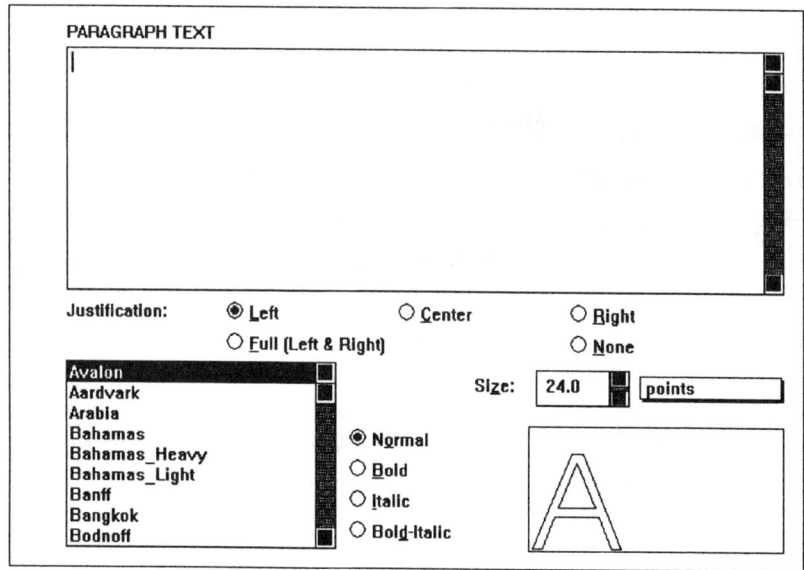

Fig. 2-2 **Text attributes dialog box ('paragraph text').**

Working with text: Creating new text

Cursor movement controls, once you have text in the box

- **Cursor control arrows**, work as normal, moving the cursor through the text, left and right and up and down

- **Page Up**, moves the cursor directly to the first line of the text

- **Page Down**, moves the cursor directly to the last line of text displayed in the 'window'

- **Home**, moves the cursor to the beginning of the line it is on

- **End**, moves the cursor to the end of the line it is on.

Using the mouse in the text window

If you want to move the cursor quickly to a particular place in the text – say, to amend or add a character – do this:

1 Start by keying-in some text. Any text will do. All you need is a few characters and spaces and a couple of blank lines, then some more text.

2 Move the screen pointer onto the text window and you will see the pointer change shape into what looks like a little hat stand. This is your text pointer.

Let us say that you want to delete a particular character...

Working with text:
Amending new text

1 Choose the character you want to delete, then move your **text pointer** to the gap, or space before it, and tap **Delete**. (Alternatively you could move to the gap after the letter and tap BACKSPACE.)

If you want to get rid of a block of letters or words...

1 Move the text pointer to the gap before (or after) the block, CLICK AND HOLD and 'wipe' a band of highlighting across the text to the end (or beginning) of the block. Make sure you have highlighted all the characters you want to delete, but no more. Then tap **Delete** or BACKSPACE.

An easier and more accurate way of achieving the same end as this is to:

2 Move the **text pointer** to the gap before (or after) the block, CLICK to position the text cursor, then hold down a SHIFT key. Next, move the **text pointer** to the end (or beginning) of your chosen block and CLICK again to highlight the whole block. Finally, tap **Delete** or BACKSPACE as before.

The second method is more convenient because, if you miss the final character, or if you go one character too far, you simply hold down the SHIFT key, then move the text pointer to include or exclude the character and CLICK again to add or eliminate it.

Working with text: Cut, Copy and Paste

You quite often want to move the text around on the page by 'Cutting', or 'Copying' it from one place and 'Pasting' it into another.

1   Begin by highlighting a section of your text.

2   To **COPY** the block you have highlighted, hold down the **Ctrl** key and tap the **Insert** key. This puts a copy of the highlighted text onto the (Windows) clipboard.

3   Move the text pointer to the end of your text and (simply for this exercise) tap the **SPACEBAR**. To **PASTE**-in the text you copied, either:
(a) click on the **Paste** button at the bottom of the screen, or
(b) hold down a **SHIFT** key and tap **Insert**. In fact, try both!

So the Ctrl+Insert combination takes a copy of the text, but leaves the original where it is. And the SHIFT+Insert combination (or the Paste button) brings the text from the clipboard and places it where the text cursor is located. When you want to move a section of text from one place to another, you begin by 'cutting it, rather than copying it, before moving and pasting it, like this:

4   Highlight the text you have just pasted in, by clicking at the beginning of the block. Tap **SHIFT+Delete** to cut it. Move the screen pointer to the start of your text, **CLICK**, and then **PASTE**-in the block of text as you did just now.

Working with text:
Layout - justification

The text in the 'text entry box' is the raw material from which you will create the processed text that will appear on the page. In other words the 'creation' of the text and the 'setting' of the text are two separate stages. In the first stage you concentrate on getting the basic words right and in the second you work on making it look right.

To make the text 'look right' you will want to control a number of variables. For the moment we can regard these variables as being of two types: firstly, the layout of the text – where and how it appears on the page – and secondly, the attributes of the text – the typeface, the style, the size and so on. In this section we shall look at the layout of text.

By the time you get to the text entry dialog box you will have already made certain decisions about the text you want to create. For example, whether it should be string or paragraph text and roughly **where** it should appear on the page. But this dialog box allows you to take that process a little further, by specifying **how** it should be laid out in the location you have chosen.

As you can see in Figure 2-3, part of the dialog box allows you to determine the 'justification', or 'vertical alignment' of the text. You will see that you have five little 'radio' buttons which control this. If you look in the bottom left hand corner of the dialog box on your screen, you will see you can also control the spacing of the text (but more about that shortly). Let us first look at 'justification'.

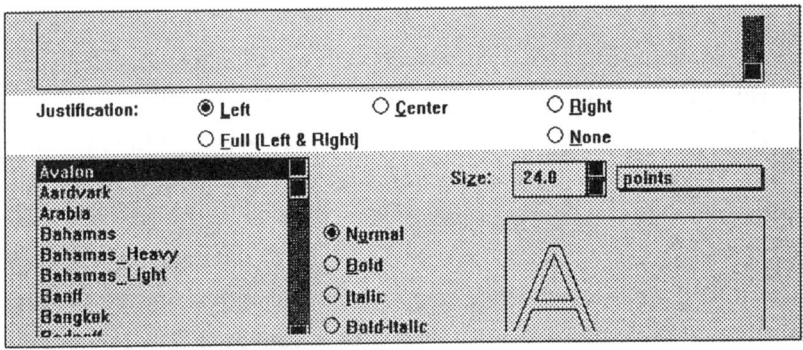

Fig. 2-3 **Layout controls – text entry dialog box.**

The top three buttons are labelled: **Left, Center** (sic) and **Right**. You can select these buttons in the normal way with the mouse, or by tapping Alt plus a letter key. On this dialog box, and all the others, when you see a letter underlined in one of the labels, it means, 'hold down the Alt key and tap this letter to select this option'.

The **Left** option lines up all the text down its left hand side. In the jargon, it 'ranges the text left'; the **Center** option ranges the text about its centre line; and the **Right** option ranges the text right. **Full**, which is not available for string text (that was one of the small differences between the dialog boxes we mentioned earlier), ranges the text both right and left. And the **None** option, though available on the paragraph text dialog box, is really designed to help you adjust the size and position of individual characters in string text.

Working with text:
Layout - justification

It is all very well to talk blithely about ranging text to the left, or the centre or the right, and it is easy enough to visualise when you are working with paragraph text (you simply range to the margins of the bounding box you create). But, to what exactly are you ranging string text!? Have a look at the diagrams below and you will see the difference between the two types of text.

The dotted line in the string text illustration represents the vertical position of the crosshairs when you click on the page. The two dotted lines in the paragraph text illustration represent the two sides of the bounding box you draw to select paragraph text. So remember, string text is ranged relative to where you clicked on the page, while paragraph text is ranged to the left, right or centre of the bounding box.

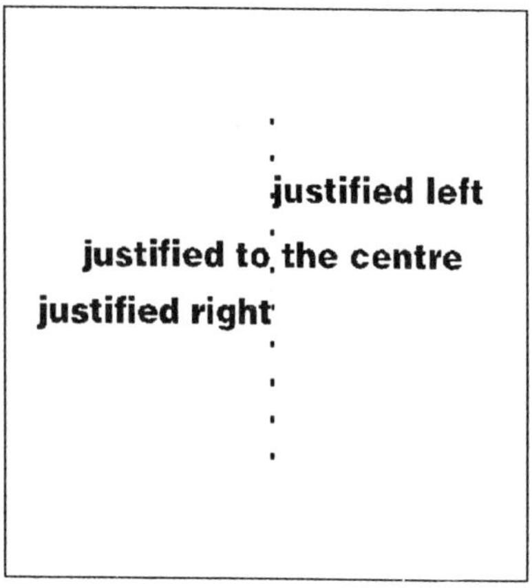

Fig. 2-4   **Text alignment 'string text'.**

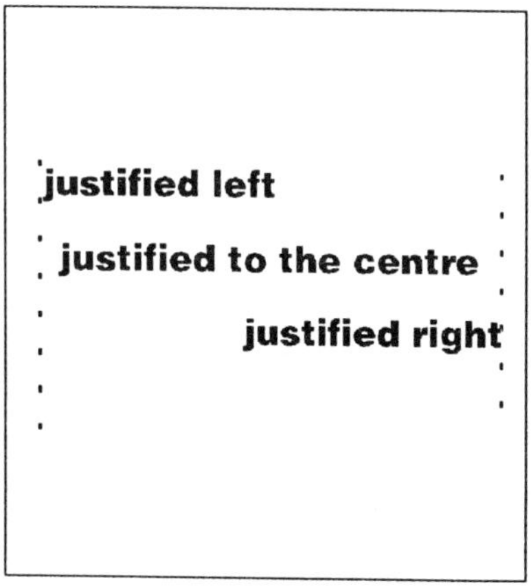

Fig. 2-5   **Text alignment 'paragraph text'.**

Working with text:
Layout - spacing

1   CLICK on the button labelled **Spacing**, at the bottom left hand corner of the dialog box (or tap 'Alt+S').

CD! displays a further dialog box which you can also see illustrated in Figure 2-6. These are the settings which give you fine control over the spacing between individual characters, between words, between lines of text (those which CD! 'wraps around' automatically) and between paragraphs (where you have forced the end of a line by tapping RETURN). The standard inter-character and inter-word settings should be fine for most occasions, but you may well want to play around with the inter-line and the inter-paragraph settings.

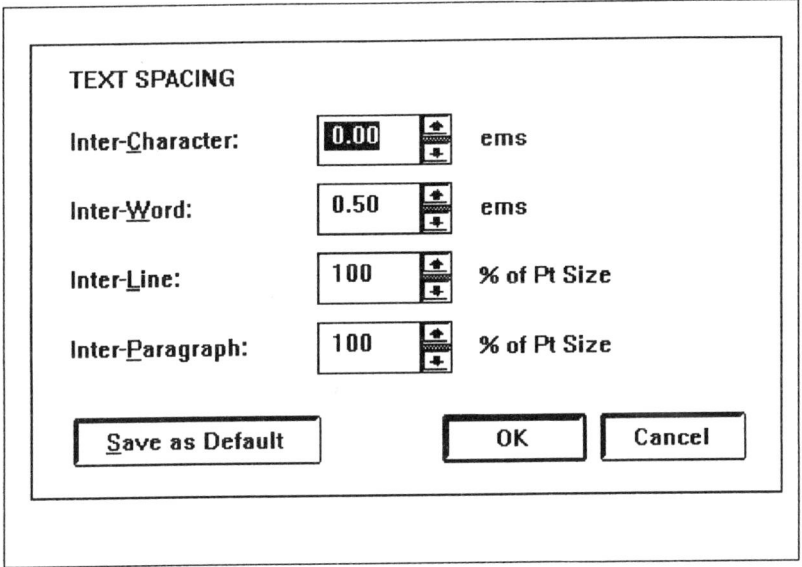

Fig. 2-6   **Text spacing dialog box.**

Working with text:
Layout - spacing

In CD! you have to tap RETURN twice to make a new paragraph. CD! treats any text which is preceded by a blank line as being a new paragraph. But that does not mean that the space between paragraphs has to be twice the distance between successive lines of text. You may not want the inter-paragraph spacing to be twice as big as the spaces between lines; it can sometimes look a little blocky and unpleasing, but more importantly, the line and paragraph spacing are tools you can use to maximise the visual effect and the information content of a block of text. Take the text here as an example.

The text in this column is set like the rest of the book.	In this column the text has been set with the same word and character spacing.
The spacings between lines and between paragraphs are set to different multiples of the type size.	But we have changed the line and paragraph spacing. There are 29 words and two carriage returns in the other column and 46 words and two carriage return in this one.

For example, try setting the line spacing to, say 100% of the type size and the paragraph spacing to 50%. We think it gives quite a pleasing result. Once you have found a setting you like, you can make it the standard one by clicking on the 'Save as Default' button. N.B. You will not be able to amend the inter-paragraph spacing for string text. Altering the line spacing will do the job for you, though.

Working with text:
Typeface and Style

1 Delete any text you might have in the text entry box.

Your screen should now look like the one in Figure 2-7. For our purposes here, there are four things to look at in this illustration and on your screen:

- the typeface selector

- the type style preview box

- the type style selector

- the type size selector.

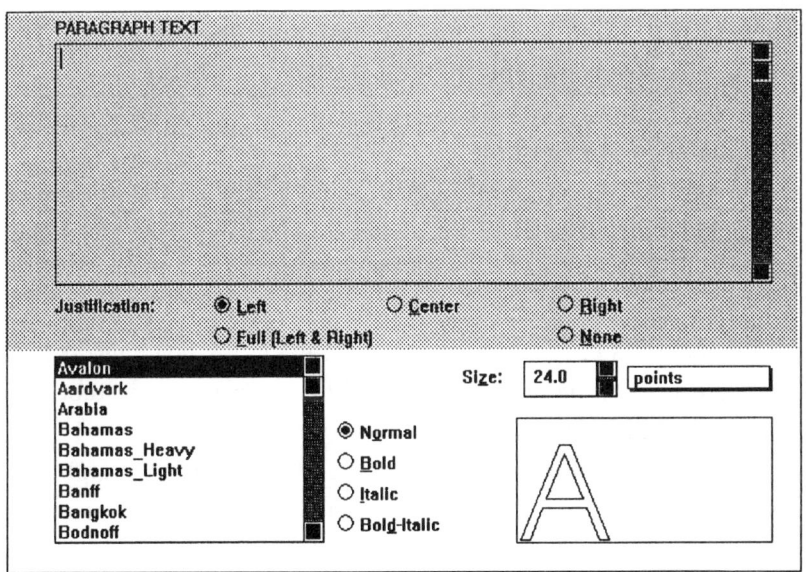

Fig. 2-7 **Typeface, Style and Size settings.**

Working with text: Typeface and Style

The typeface selector

is at the left of your screen. CD! offers you a list of 75 type 'families' – you can see only nine of them in the 'list window' at any one time. To see the full list of what is available, you scroll the list, either by clicking and holding on the 'slider' control (just below the upward facing arrow on the right hand side of the window) and then dragging the slider slowly downward. Or you can achieve the same result by clicking, or clicking-and-holding, on the downward and upward facing arrows (located above and below the slider control). All 'list windows' in CD! work like this (because it is running in Windows 3).

You select a typeface for your text by clicking on the name of the typeface you want to use for the text you are processing. Try selecting the **Aardvark** typeface (near the top of the list).

The type style preview box

at the right of the screen changes to show you what the **outline** of the capitalised first letter of the alphabet of that typeface looks like. We need to make a couple of points about this.

(a) This happens only when you have no text in the text entry box. If you have text in the entry box, CD! shows you what the first two characters of the text will look like in the typeface.

(b) We used the expression 'the capitalised first letter of the alphabet' rather than the words, 'a capital A', quite deliberately. Try selecting the typeface called **Musical_Symbols**, or the one called **Dixieland** to see why.

Working with text:
Typeface and Style

The type style selector

is the column of radio buttons in the middle of the screen. When you select Dixieland typeface you will notice that it is available only in 'normal' style. Most, but not all, of the typefaces are available in normal style, many are available in normal plus one or more others, some are available in all four styles, while, for example, **ZurichCalligraphic** is available only in italic style and **Aardvark** is available only in bold.

1   Scroll back to the start of the list and select **Avalon.**

You will see that the labels for all four radio buttons are in black lettering. This tells you that all four styles are available to you.

2   Select **Aardvark** and look at the radio buttons.

You will see that only the word Bold is in black. All the other labels are in grey lettering. Only bold style is available to you.

3   Select **Avalon** again and then **CLICK** on each of the four radio buttons in turn, while you keep an eye on the typeface preview box. It will illustrate the differences between the different type styles for this typeface.

Working with text: Typeface and Style

The type size selector

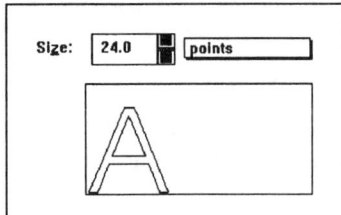

is located just above the type style preview box. Here you can see that the type size for text you create now will be 24 points. With 72 points to the inch, it means the text will be one third of an inch high on the page.

1 CLICK on the word **points** and you will see it change to 'inches' and the figures change to 0.33 (approximately one third of an inch, as we said). CLICK again and you get the measurement 8.5 millimeters (sic). CLICK once more and you get 2,0 picas, point. CLICK one final time to cycle round to points again.

So you can set the size of your text with any one of four measurement systems. You change the actual size in either of two ways.

1 To make a relatively small change, you can click on the up or down arrows in the size window. CLICK on the **up arrow** a few times. You will see the size increase, in this case, by one point at a time. If you click and hold on one of the arrows the numbers will scroll up or down quickly to the number you want.

2 To make a change more quickly, CLICK on the **numbers** to activate a cursor, then delete the existing numbers and key-in, say, the number 72.00 to make the text an inch tall.

Working with text:
Putting the text on the page

There are just two more items (other than OK and Cancel) on the paragraph text dialog box which we have not examined: Two buttons, one labelled **Columns...** and the other labelled **Import...**, you will see them at the bottom of your screen.

Columns...

If you want to lay the text out in more than one column (you can have up to eight) you would click on this button. Try it now. CD! presents you with a dialog box which allows you to specify two settings:

- '# of Columns (number of columns)

- Gutter Width (in CD! and in other DTP programs, the 'gutter' is the space between columns).

You adjust the numbers in the same way you adjusted the size settings just now. (There are the same four measurement systems for setting the width of the gutter.)

Import...

When you click on this button, CD! expects you to import an ASCII text file (see the glossary) which you have created with some other writing package (e.g. your normal word processor). It displays a dialog box in which you have to specify the filename and 'path' (where the file is on the hard disc). It assumes at first that the file will be called something dot (full stop) txt, but you can change this. You simply key-in the name of the file you want to import and then click on Import to put the file into the text entry box at the cursor position.

Working with text:
Putting the text on the page

The Columns... and Import... buttons are not active when you are generating string text – for fairly obvious reasons. And that is the other difference between generating paragraph and string text we mentioned a while ago.

So now we have seen all the settings on the dialog box. Let us use some of them to get some text on the page.

1   If you have text in the text entry box, delete it. Now key-in: **Wordplay**, make sure that the size is set to **72 points**, select the **Aardvark** type face, choose **Center** justification and then, at long last, **CLICK** on **OK**. (Remember, tapping RETURN won't work on this dialog box.)

At 72 points (72pt), the word 'Wordplay' is just over four and a half inches wide on the page. Of course, we don't know the size of the rectangle you drew way back on page 75 when we generated the paragraph bounding box, so if you cannot see the whole word on one line, or if you get nothing at all in the bounding box do this:

1   Tap the **SPACEBAR** to select the Pick tool. Grab the bottom right sizing handle and expand the box. **RELEASE** the handle and see if the word fits now. If not, expand the box a little more until it does fit.

Now we can begin to use CD! to play around with the text!

Working with text: Making adjustments

The colour, position and shape of text

1   CLICK the **right mouse button** to see a full page preview of the text you have on your screen. See what you think and then CLICK it again to get back to the work page.

2   If you haven't already done so, select the **Pick tool**.

The text you had on screen in the preview, looked fat and black and heavy – like a plumber's wallet – but we can change it. Some of the changes are a bit subtle, so it will help us if we generate another copy of the same text for comparison. Once again we can do that in a couple of ways, but the easiest for us at the moment is to just generate the same text again, with the same settings.

1   Move the existing text to near the top left hand corner of the page. (**CLICK AND HOLD** on the outline of the bounding box, then drag the box to its new position.)

2   Now tap **Ctrl+D** to duplicate the selected object (i.e. your text).

You will see two versions of the box now, slightly offset from each other. The upper box – offset to the right – is the duplicate (not that it matters here, because they are both the same and their precise positions are not critical, but it might be important to know that in some situations as we shall see in a moment).

Working with text:
Making adjustments

We need to separate the two images so we can see them more clearly. But before we do that, let us show you a simple effect.

1   CLICK on the **Outlines** pen nib icon. When you get the fly-out menu, CLICK on the sixth icon from the right in the top row.

2   Move the screen pointer down to the palette at the bottom of the screen and, with the RIGHT **mouse button,** CLICK on the colour white. (You may have to scroll the palette to get the white tablet on screen. CLICK on the left hand **scroll arrow** until the white tablet appears at the left hand end of the palette.) Then move the screen pointer back onto the work page and get a full page preview by clicking the RIGHT **mouse button** again.

You can expand this image and this effect by duplicating the new image as many times as you like. This is what it looks like when we made three more duplications. The image here is a little coarse, because it is a screen dump ('snapshot' of the screen). The printed image would be of much higher quality. Even so, you can see the effect.

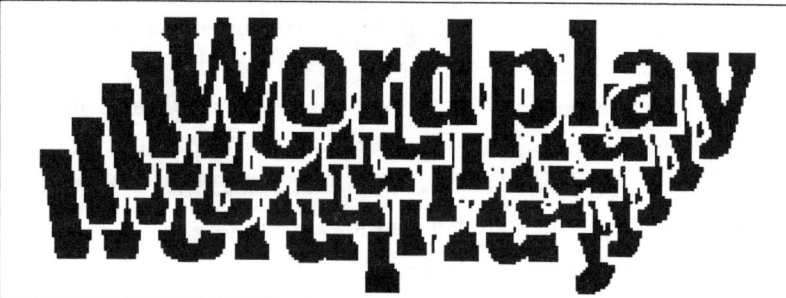

Working with text: Making adjustments

3   CLICK the RIGHT **mouse button** again to get back to the work page. Then CLICK AND HOLD on the **bounding box** of the duplicate text (the upper right one) and drag the outline down to place it neatly below the original text. RELEASE the click to fix the text in this position.

Remember we made an adjustment to the outline of the duplicate, so the two copies of the text are slightly different. We need to make them the same.

4   CLICK on the outline of the upper box (the original). Now, as before, CLICK on the **Outlines** pen nib icon. When you get the fly-out menu, CLICK on the sixth icon from the right in the top row. Then move the screen pointer down to the palette at the bottom of the screen and, with the RIGHT **mouse button**, CLICK on the colour white.

(See page 226 for a quicker way of doing this.) We now have two exact copies of the same text, so it doesn't matter which one we work on to experiment with various effects. Let us first of all deal with colour.

1   Adjust the palette (by clicking on the scroll arrows) so the white tablet is at the left of the palette you can see on screen. Then RIGHT CLICK (i.e. 'click the right mouse button') on the deep blue tablet and CLICK (normally) on the bright red tablet. Finally get a full screen preview.

Working with text:
Making adjustments

Repeat the experiment with different colour combinations until you get an effect you like. You can make adjustments to the text with another tool, but we want to skip those until we look at that tool itself in more detail (see pp 135-144 for the main discussion). We can, however, look now at one straightforward way of making adjustments to the text in the box. The upper box should still be selected for processing.

1 Tap **Ctrl+T** and wait for a moment. CD! will present you with the Text Entry Dialog Box you filled-in when you created your text.

You can now change any or all of the settings you specified earlier. We shall change two of them; the typeface and the type size. (Incidentally, because of the typefaces we have chosen to use in this example, the type style will change automatically as well.)

2 Scroll the type face list to the very bottom and select **ZurichCalligraphic.**

3 Even though we have not changed the point size (yet) this typeface will look a lot smaller on the page, so to compensate we <u>will</u> change the point size to **108 points.** When you have made the change, CLICK on OK.

4 You will probably have to change the size of the text bounding box. So do that next. Then get a page preview.

Working with text: Making adjustments

So far we have been working with paragraph text. When you work with string text the procedures are slightly different.

1 Begin by selecting the **Text tool** again.

2 Position the crosshairs just below the 'W' of '**Wordplay**' in the lower bounding box, leaving plenty of room below the box. **CLICK** on the page to get the text entry dialog box.

3 Key-in the word, **Wordplay** again. **CLICK** on the radio button for **left justification,** leave all the other settings the same and then **CLICK** on **OK.**

You will notice immediately that when you create string text, it appears on the page in the actual typeface you selected. There are a couple of good reasons for this. Firstly, you will usually have a lot less string text than paragraph text on the page, so CD! will have to spend less time updating the image. Secondly, you would normally use string text when you want to create an impact, so CD! gives you much more control over the image – the outline – of the text. We can see that now:

1 Start by getting a page preview, just to fix the image in your mind. Then select the **Pick tool**. Then select one of the paragraph text bounding boxes and stretch it to the right.

Working with text:
Making adjustments

When you stretch the bounding box of paragraph text it does not alter the text itself. You will see the text move slightly to range either side of the new centre line of the stretched box, but that is all.

2 Now select the string text (by clicking on the outline of a letter) and try stretching it to the right. Try stretching it downwards as well.

You will see the text behave just like all the objects we created with the drawing tools in part one of the book. You use precisely the same controls. Just for devilment, try flipping the image, by holding down the Ctrl key and shrinking the image past its zero point. Try holding down a SHIFT key while stretching and shrinking the image...

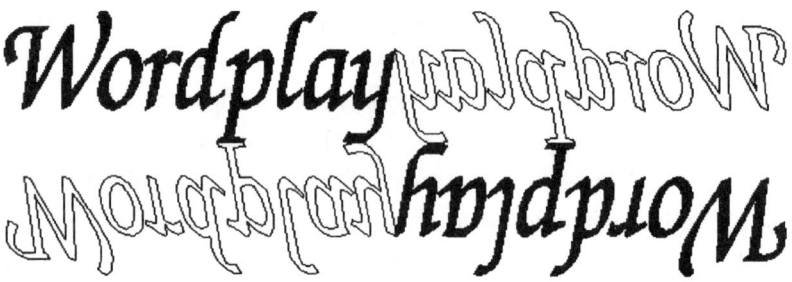

If you can stretch and mirror the image, it means you can move it. It means you can change the colour and thickness of the lines and you can change the fills (as we have here). In short it means that you can treat string text like any other closed object.

You will see how significant this is as we look at the other tools.

Working with text: Symbols

CD! comes with a wide selection of symbols. You can generate these symbols and treat them like any other object. In fact, using symbols is very like using string text and just as easy.

1   Select the **Text** tool **icon**, then hold down a SHIFT key and CLICK in the middle of the page.

After a moment or two, CD! presents you with the dialog box which looks like the one in Figure 2-8. Yours may not look exactly the same. Let us explore the various components of the dialog box, just in case it isn't clear what the different items are for.

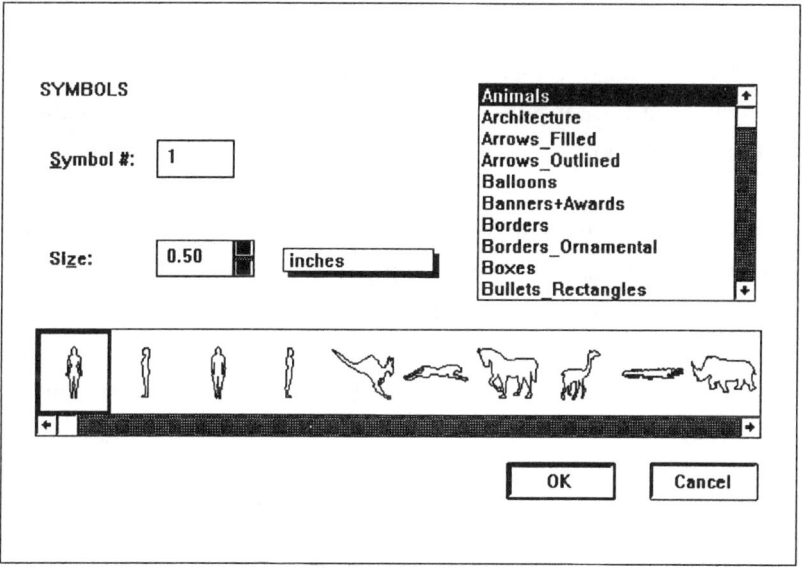

Fig. 2-8   **The Symbols dialog box.**

Working with text: Symbols

On the right hand side at the top you have a list window, which contains the names of 39 different sets of symbols. You can see that in the illustration the set called 'Animals' is selected. You make your selection from this list window in precisely the same way you made a selection from the typeface list.

When you select a set, CD! displays ten of the symbols from the set in the long strip across the lower part of the dialog box. You make your selection of the particular symbol you want, either by clicking on its image and then tapping RETURN or clicking on OK. Or, if you know its reference number, by keying that number into the box at the top left of the dialog box – the box labelled 'Symbol #:' and then tapping RETURN or clicking on OK. You can tell when a symbol is selected, because it has a black rectangle around it. In the illustration, the symbol at the far left of the strip is selected and this happens to be the first symbol in the animals set – ladies first.

If you want to review the symbols in a set, the long strip has scroll buttons and a scroll slider bar to help you pan through what's available. With some sets it will take some time, because they contain lots of symbols. E.g. the 'Dixieland' and 'Geographic Symbols' sets each contain more than 250 symbols. Suffice it to say that you have several symbols to choose from.

1 Select the **Animals** set and make sure that the scroll slider bar is at the left hand end of its travel and **CLICK** on the image of the **jaguar** (number 6 in this set).

Working with text: Symbols

2   Next, adjust the size of the image by editing the number in the box labelled **Si̱ze:** – just above the preview strip. Make the image **3 inches** square (here again, you have four measurement systems to choose from). Finally **CLICK** on **OK** to put the image on the work page.

Now we can play about with the symbol, just as with any other closed object.

1   Tap the **SPACEBAR** to select the **Pick tool**. Now stretch the image by dragging on the corner handles. You will remember that this stretches the image without changing its aspect ratio.

2   Next grab the lower side handle and make the image just a little fatter.

You should end up with an image like this one bounding across the page. CD!'s built-in symbols give you great flexibility ... and don't forget you also got other Clipart libraries with your copy of CD!.

Take some time to play around with symbols before you move on.

PART THREE
Shaping and Adjusting Objects

Adjusting Shapes: The Zoom tool

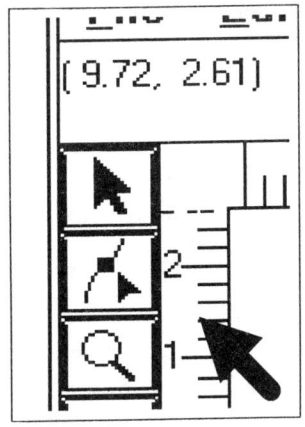

Fig. 3-1 **Tools for adjusting shapes.**

In reality only two of the tools in this set of three are for adjusting shapes. The other one simply enables you to do it more easily.

Starting from the top we have the Pick tool, which you have already used quite a lot. Then there is the Shaping tool and lastly the Zoom tool. We shall start this part of the book by looking at the Zoom tool, because we shall need to use it while we are looking at the other two. You select this tool just like any other.

1   Start by drawing a rectangle on the page, make it quite small. Then **CLICK** on the little picture of a magnifying glass to get a fly-out menu, which looks like this.

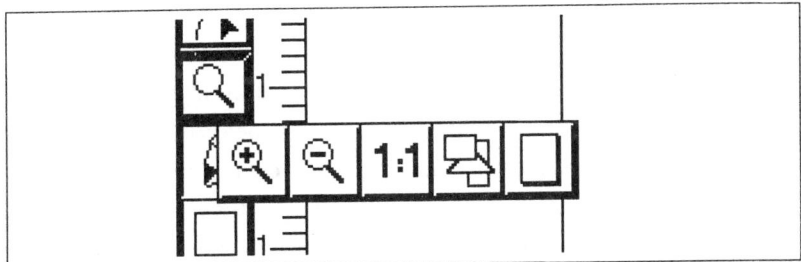

Fig. 3-2 **The Zoom tool fly-out menu.**

Adjusting Shapes:
The Zoom tool

You can also use F keys to select the zoom-in and zoom-out functions. In fact, you can use a range of F keys to select tools. (See Section Six, Quick Reference.)

Just before we use the tool, have a look at your work screen. You can probably see the whole work page, with its drop shadow and you can see the rectangle you drew. Remember this configuraton.

1   Move the screen pointer to the fly-out menu and **CLICK** on the first icon, the **magnifying glass with a +** sign. Move back onto the work page and you will see that the screen pointer has changed to look like the icon you just selected.

2   Position the pointer so it is above and to the left of the top left corner of the rectangle you drew. **CLICK AND HOLD** and drag out an elastic rectangle as in Figure 3-3.

3   When you have enclosed the part of the image you want to zoom-in on, **RELEASE** the click.

CD! will try to fill the screen with the area you indicated, but the size of the image you get depends a bit on the shape of the rectangle you pulled out with the Zoom-in tool. Certainly everything you enclosed in the 'marquee' will be enlarged on screen, but, put crudely, the smaller the marquee you draw and the closer its aspect ratio is to that of the work screen, the bigger the magnification.

Adjusting Shapes: The Zoom tool

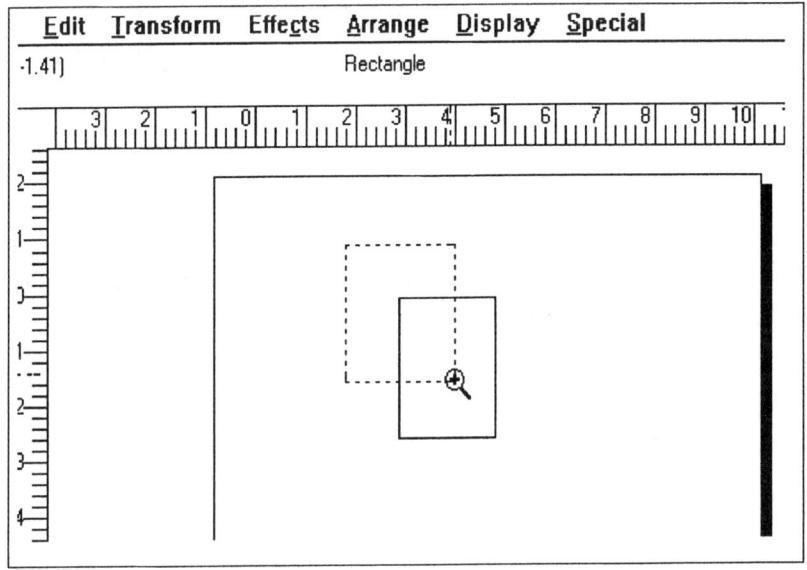

Fig. 3-3 **Zooming in on one corner of a rectangle.**

You can zoom-in further, by selecting the Zoom-in tool again and repeating the process you went through just now. This time, rather than shuffling the screen pointer about all over the place, we'll use the shortcut method of selecting the tool.

1 Tap **F2**. The screen pointer changes shape to tell you that you have selected the Zoom-in tool. Enlarge the top left hand corner of the rectangle again, by dragging out another marquee and then **RELEASING** ... **Repeat** the process **twice** more.

Adjusting Shapes:
The Zoom tool

We can get an idea of how far we have zoomed in if we draw something at this scale and then zoom-out to the start position again, so:

1   Select the **Ellipse tool**, then hold down SHIFT+CONTROL and draw out a circle centred on the corner of the rectangle.

2   Tap F3 to zoom-out back out one step, then repeat the process until you get back to the position in Figure 3-3, i.e. back to where we came in, with the whole work page on screen. Then select a full page preview to get a clear view of the little circle you drew.

So F2 activates the Zoom-in tool and you can repeat its use up to 20 times in one sequence. (The maximum magnification you can get, depends ultimately on the hardware that drives your monitor).

F3 zooms-out one step in the zoom sequence you carried out. But you can get back to the work page in one go from a zoom, like this:

1   Begin by zooming in on your little circle again. Go in at least three steps. When you have done that, CLICK on the **Zoom tool icon**.

2   At the extreme right of the fly-out menu you will see an icon which represents a page. In fact it represents your work page. CLICK on the **Page icon** and watch your screen.

Adjusting Shapes:
The Zoom tool

You go straight back to the work page in one step. Incidentally, you can implement this command with an F key combination as well; **SHIFT+F4** does the job equally well and it is easier to call-up.

3   CLICK on the **Zoom tool icon** again and we can have a quick look at all the options and the shortcut codes.

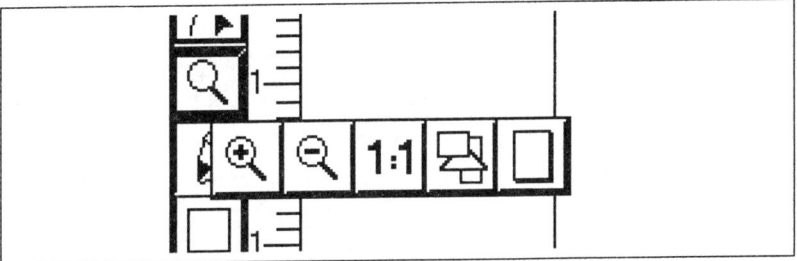

Fig. 3-4   **The Zoom tool fly-out menu.**

The magnifying glass with a + symbol = zoom-in – code **F2**.
The magnifying glass with a - symbol = zoom-out a step – code **F3**.

The **1:1** option causes CD! to display the image at the actual size it will be on the page (or as near to it as the computer hardware and software can manage). No code for this option (as far as we can tell).

The next option, with an icon representing various objects, will give you a display in which your objects fill the work screen – code **F4**.

The last option gets you back to your normal work page – code **SHIFT+F4**.

Adjusting Shapes:
The Zoom tool

You will find the zoom options invaluable when you work with CD!, particularly when you have to position objects very accurately or when you are making tiny, but important, adjustments to an image.

Here again it is worthwhile taking the time to play around with the controls before you move on. Notice that you can scroll your image, no matter what its magnification, using the scroll controls at the right and at the bottom of the work screen. If you have set up the rulers on your screen, as we have, you will notice that their scale changes as you zoom in and out, so you are always able to size objects accurately. You can see it here, where we have zoomed in on the little circle in our image. Notice how big the ruler scale is.

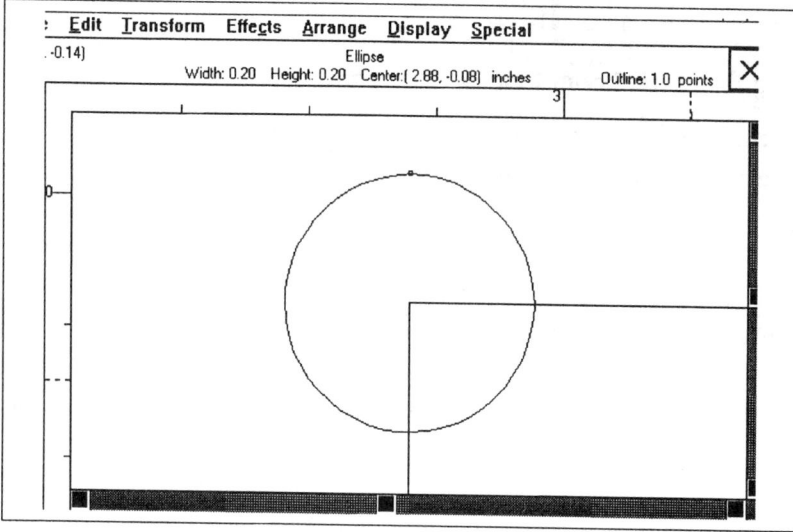

Fig. 3-5 **Rulers changing scale with the zoom.**

Adjusting Shapes:
More about the Pick tool

If you have worked straight through from the previous section you will have two objects on screen: a rectangle and a little circle. If you do not have these objects on screen, please create them as you did when you worked through the pages before.

1 Select the **Pick tool**. Draw a marquee which encloses both objects and thereby selects them both for processing.

Moving objects
Basic method
You have already seen the basic principles of moving objects on screen, so before we look at some refinements to the basic process, let us remind ourselves of how it works.

1 To move the selected object(s) from one place to another on the page, position the screen pointer so it is on, or very close to, the outline of the object – in our case, to the outline of either one of the two objects selected for processing.

'...Very close to...' in this instance means not more than 5 'pixels' (basic picture elements) away from the outline. You can see the settings for your system by tapping Ctrl+J to select the Preferences option from the Special menu ... and then clicking on the Lines & Curves... button to generate a list of the Tracking, Threshold and Autojoin settings. See also Figure 1-4.

Adjusting Shapes:
More about the Pick tool

2   CLICK AND HOLD with the pointer on the outline and then drag a blue 'shadow' rectangle to one side, clear of the original image, then RELEASE the click to place the objects.

Constraining the move

1   CLICK AND HOLD on one of the outlines again (if you miss and de-select the objects, re-select both objects with a marquee select). Now hold down the **Ctrl** key and try dragging the objects. You will be able to move the shadow rectangle only vertically or horizontally.

Moving and leaving the original behind

1   As before, CLICK AND HOLD on one of the outlines. Start to move the shadow rectangle and (still holding the left mouse button down) CLICK the **right mouse button** (or tap **grey +**). Position the shadow rectangle and then RELEASE the left mouse button. You will have two copies of the objects, the original in the original location and your copy in the new location. Try repeating this with the **Ctrl**, constrain key, held down as well.

'Nudging' an image into position

1   With the objects selected, tap the cursor arrow keys and watch the objects move in small increments with each tap.

Adjusting Shapes:
More about the Pick tool

Note

You can set the size of each 'nudge increment' by tapping Ctrl+J for the Preferences dialog box. On our system (and probably on yours) Nudge is set to 0.10 inches, but you can set to whatever suits you best.

In Part 2 we had a go at flipping the image of some paragraph text, but you will know that you can flip any image easily by shrinking it past its zero point while holding down the Ctrl key. You don't have to hold down the Ctrl key to flip the image, but remember that Ctrl constrains the stretch and shrink operation to multiples of the starting size of the objects. So holding down Ctrl merely ensures that when the image does flip, it will be exactly the same size as the original.

Flipping an image and leaving the original behind

1   Tidy up the work page by deleting all but one copy of our objects. Then, marquee select both objects.

2   If your image is near the bottom of the page, move it upwards so it is quite near the top.

3   **Grab** the **top side handle** and start shrinking the object slowly. Now tap the **+ key on the number pad** (the one on the main keyboard won't work for this), then hold down **Ctrl**.

Adjusting Shapes:
More about the Pick tool

4   Keep shrinking the image until it flips and then **RELEASE the mouse button before** letting go of **Ctrl**.

Tapping the number pad + key works whenever you are stretching and scaling. If you use it in conjunction with other key combinations we have seen, you can get effects like these fairly simple examples.

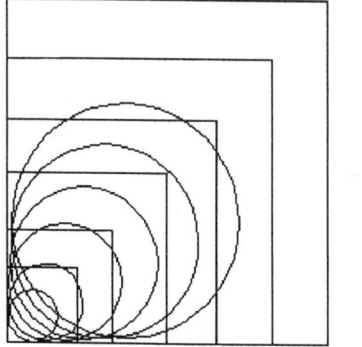 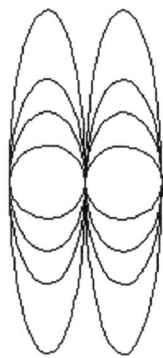

These are screen shots from our system of some shapes we produced in a matter of seconds. For someone with a bit more time and a little more artistic talent, the possibilities are endless.

You now have four objects on screen with the Pick tool still active. Two of the objects are selected for processing.

1   De-select the objects by clicking on a blank part of the page.

Remember, the Pick tool is still active, even though nothing is selected.

Adjusting Shapes:
More about the Pick tool

Selecting individual objects

When you have several objects on screen and you want to process just one of them, say to change its fill or its outline, you can select that one object in a couple of ways:

1 Move the screen pointer to the outline of the lower little circle and **CLICK** to select it. If the little circle is really very little, then you might need to zoom-in a couple of steps to make the image bigger before you select it. Once it is selected zoom-out to the whole page display with **SHIFT+F4**.

Sometimes it is easier to select an individual object in a different way, like this:

2 Tap the **Tab** key **four times** and watch the screen.

Each time you tap the Tab key CD! selects an individual object and you can cycle through the whole set until you get to the one you want.

Selecting some objects, but not all

1 With the lower circle selected, hold down a **SHIFT** key, move the screen pointer onto the outline of the lower box and **CLICK** to select two objects of the four. Then tap **Delete**.

Adjusting Shapes:
More about the Pick tool

You will now have your two original objects on screen: a rectangle and a little circle. If you do not have these objects on screen, please create them as you did when you worked through the pages before.

1 Marquee select both objects for processing, then move them to the top of the work page.

2 Move the screen pointer to the **outline of one of the objects** (not the sizing handles). Make sure the arrow pointer is on, or at least very close to, the outline, make sure you keep the mouse still and **CLICK** once more. You should get a result like the one shown in Figure 3-6.

You will see there are two different kinds of arrow on screen. The curved ones, at the corners, control the rotation of the object(s), while the straight arrows by each side control the skew of the object(s). The arrows are a bit like the sizing handles you get when you select objects, but they have a different function. Notice that the image on screen also has, right in the centre, a circle with a dot in the middle. That dot is the centre of rotation. Let us see how this mode works.

Rotating an image

1 Move your screen pointer to the **curved arrow at the bottom left** of the image. **Grab** that arrow, as you would a sizing handle and then **push gently upwards**.

Adjusting Shapes:
More about the Pick tool

You will see a blue shadow rectangle, bounding the image, rotate in a clockwise direction about the centre point of the image.

2   Now hold down the **Ctrl** key to constrain the movement to fixed angles and when the blue rectangle snaps into a horizontal and vertical alignment, **RELEASE** the mouse button, **then** the **Ctrl** key.

3   Now move the screen pointer to the centre point marker, **CLICK AND HOLD** on it, then drag the marker to the **bottom left corner of the work page**.

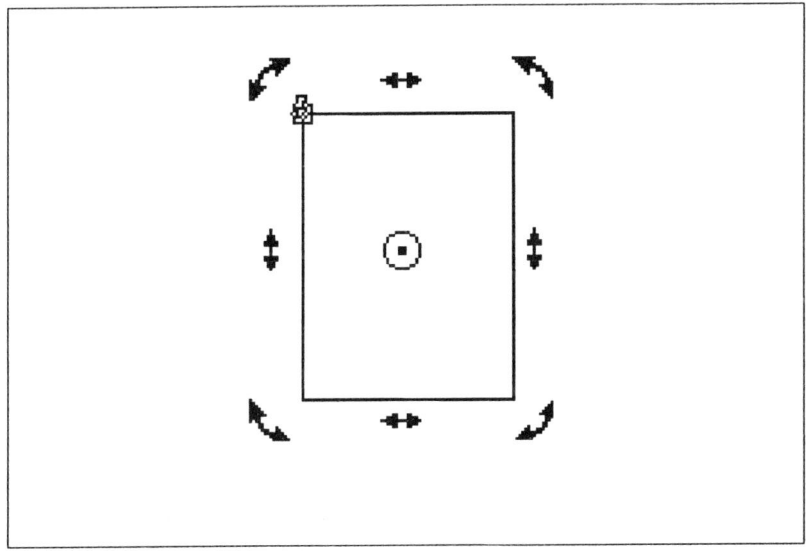

Fig. 3-6   **Rotate and skew mode selected.**

Adjusting Shapes:
More about the Pick tool

4 Grab the rotation arrow which is now at the top right corner of the image, hold down the **Ctrl** key and move the mouse downward. You will see the shadow rectangle rotate in steps as before, but this time it rotates about the new centre of rotation – at the bottom left of the page. When the shadow rectangle is standing on one corner near the bottom of the page, fix it in position there.

Notice the configuration of the arrows now. The rotation arrows are no longer by the corners of the object rectangle. They are actually at the corners of a 'notional rectangle' which encompasses the new image. This means it is very difficult to get back to the original when you rotate (or skew) your image. So always double check before releasing the mouse button.

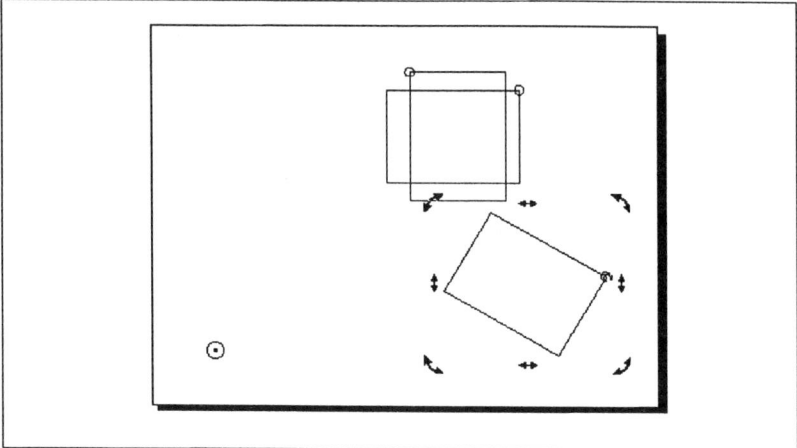

Fig. 3-7 **Rotations about different centre points.**

Adjusting Shapes:
More about the Pick tool

Skewing images

1 **Grab** the skewing arrows at the top of the new image, move the mouse gently to the left and you will see the outline of the blue rectangle start to lean leftwards. Without letting go of the mouse button, tap the **number pad +** key, then hold down the **Ctrl** key and keep moving gently left until the rectangle snaps into a new position. Then RELEASE the mouse button **before** letting go of the **Ctrl** key.

Repeat the process to get a result like this.

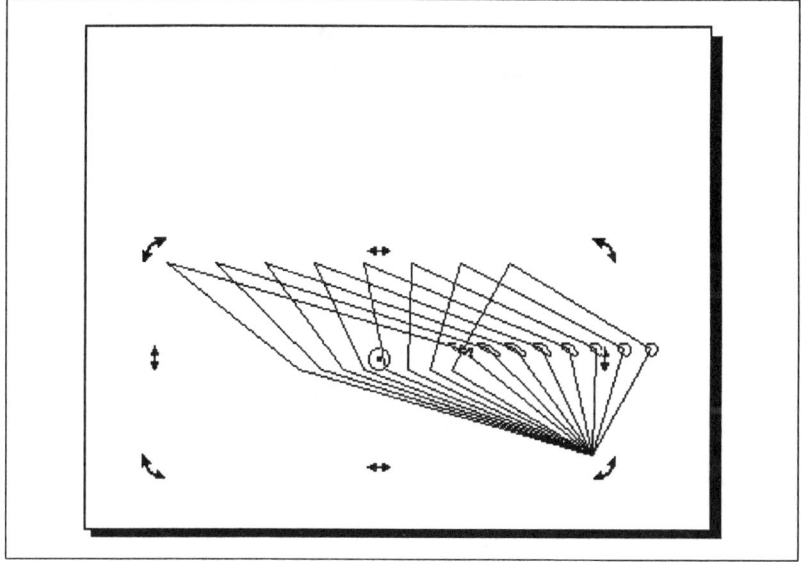

Fig. 3-8 **Successive skewing of the same image.**

Adjusting text
with the Pick tool

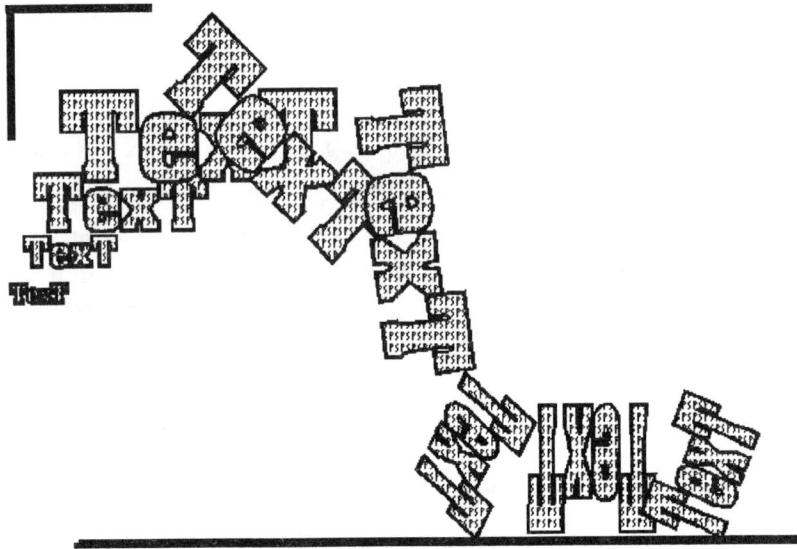

With text you can get the same effects as you can with other objects. This graphic sums them all up in one image. You just have to treat text as an object ...

There are many other effects you can apply to text, but this illustration shows the ones you can get with the Pick tool. All we did here to get the picture, was use the techniques we have been examining in the last few pages – stretch, rotate (leaving the original behind), shrink and skew (leaving the original behind).

CD! makes it all very easy to do. But you can adjust the shape of text and objects in several other ways with the Shaping tool and we shall look at that next.

Adjusting Shapes: The Shaping tool

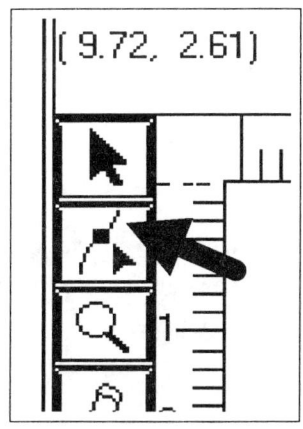

Fig. 3-9
Shaping tool icon.

The adjustments we have been making with the Pick tool, although quite impressive sometimes, have not altered the basic shapes of the objects we have been working with – a rectangle is still essentially a rectangle even when it is squashed and skewed into a bizarre contortion.

But on occasions you will want to change the basic shape of an object and that is where the Shaping tool comes in. With it you can alter basic shapes of objects: rectangles (and squares), ellipses (and circles), curves (and lines), as well as text. You can also use it to modify 'Bitmaps' which you may have imported from, say, Windows Paintbrush, or an image scanner.

Broadly speaking, Bitmaps are pictures which comprise a set number of picture elements. To CD! a bitmap is a single object, so when you enlarge a bitmapped image, the fixed number of picture elements are further apart and, consequently, you get a jagged image, like the one in the above illustration (which is in fact a stretched Windows Paintbrush image). On the other hand, CD!'s 'Vector Graphics' are expressed in terms of mathematical equations, so the resolution does not suffer when you stretch the image – CD! just re-calculates and re-draws at maximum resolution. Because of this difference, adjusting bitmaps is a slightly different sort of process.

Adjusting Shapes:
The Shaping tool,
rectangles and ellipses

We shall look at how to adjust the shape of rectangles and ellipses first, then we shall examine curves, text and bitmaps in turn. Before we start, we need to generate some objects to work with.

1   Clear your work page if it is not empty. Then draw a rectangle which almost fills the top left quadrant of the page, and draw a circle (ellipse) in the lower right quadrant of the page.

Shaping rectangles

1   Select the **Shaping tool** then CLICK on the **outline of the rectangle**.

You will see four nodes appear, one at each corner of the rectangle.

2   CLICK AND HOLD on the bottom right node (though any will do for this), now drag the node slowly to the left and watch the screen.

As you begin to move the pointer you will see two nodes appear at each corner of the rectangle. Between the two nodes at each corner there is a curve, giving you a rectangle with rounded corners. As you keep moving left, the radius of the corner arcs increases (see the status area) until you reach a point where you end up with, what looks like an ellipse.

Adjusting Shapes: The Shaping tool, rectangles and ellipses

Shaping ellipses

1   **CLICK** on the outline of your circle, then **CLICK AND HOLD on its single node**. Gently move the screen pointer in towards the centre of the circle and then slowly to the left.

You will see a 'pie wedge' shape appear with a node at each end of the arc.

2   Hold down the **Ctrl** key and when the wedge is a manageable size, say, 75 degrees (see the top status line), **RELEASE**.

3   **Grab the same node** again and very gently move the pointer outside the boundary of the former circle.

Now CD! produces a simple arc (without the wedge). If you move inside the circle you will get the wedge back, but:

4   Keeping outside the former circle, hold down the **Ctrl** key and when the arc reaches, say, 90 degrees (see the status line), **RELEASE**, to fix the arc in place. Then tap the **SPACEBAR** to select the object and notice where the sizing handles are – i.e. they are still around the original circle or ellipse. Remember this when you marquee select arcs or wedges!

Adjusting Shapes:
The Shaping tool,
curves

1   Begin this section by clearing your work page.

2   Select the **Lines and curves drawing tool**. If you are still drawing in Bézier mode, change to Freehand mode (by tapping **Ctrl+J**, selecting **Lines & Curves...** and then amending the settings in the dialog box).

3   Get back to your work page by clicking on the **OK** buttons and then draw a curve shaped roughly like this one.

4   Select the **Shaping tool** and you will get a result something like this. (It will look a lot tidier on your screen!)

CD! adds nodes to your curve and, if you look closely, you will see that there is a node at the start of the curve (left end in this example) and one for each change in the line's direction. But why are nodes important?

Adjusting Shapes: The Shaping tool, curve nodes

Of course you have already seen that nodes are control points which enable you to change the shape of objects, but when you are manipulating curves there are many more factors to take into account than we have seen so far.

For a start, there are three different kinds of curve nodes:

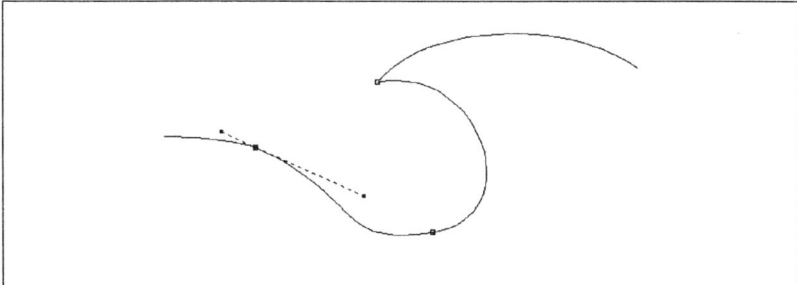

Fig. 3-10 **A 'Smooth' node.**

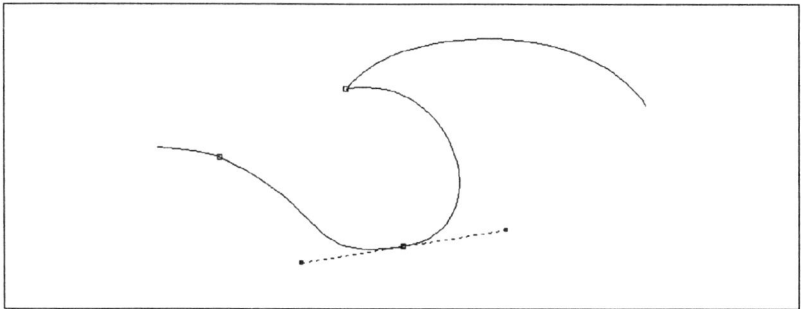

Fig. 3-11 **A 'Symmetrical' node.**

Adjusting Shapes:
The Shaping tool,
curve nodes

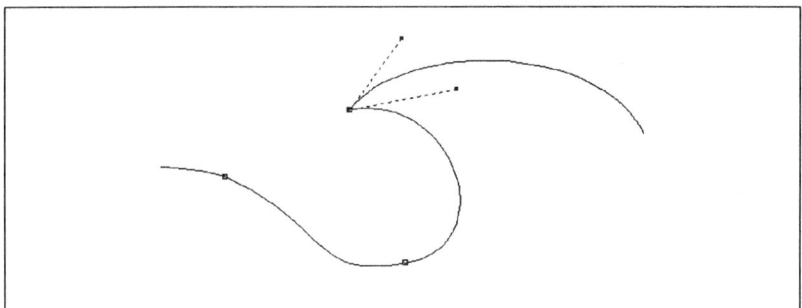

Fig. 3-12   **A 'Cusp' node.**

The three illustrations of nodes give you two types of information: Firstly, you can see at a glance the characteristics of the curve that is associated with a particular type of node. But that is because we deliberately drew the shape for that purpose. It is sometimes very difficult to tell the type of node simply from the shape of the curve it controls, which is why – when you are working on nodes – CD! always tells you which type of node you have selected.

The second type of information in the illustrations relates to the nature of the control points (or control handles) on each type of node. You can see in Figures 3-10 and 3-11 that the control handles and the node itself always lie in a straight line. But the two types of node differ in that the length of the control handles for a smooth node can be of different lengths, while for a symmetrical node they are always the same length. If you try to adjust the length of one control handle on a symmetrical node, you will actually adjust both by the same amount.

Adjusting Shapes: The Shaping tool, curve nodes

Remember that the 'height' of the curve is determined by the length of the control handles and you will see that (as in Figure 3-10) a smooth node can have differently shaped curves on either side, while a symmetrical node (Figure 3-11) has curves of the same shape on either side.

Figure 3-12 shows that the control handles for a cusp node need not be the same length and they need not lie in a straight line with the node.

So the three types of node give you three different types of control:

- with a **cusp node** you can alter the steepness and the direction of both curves at the node

- with a **smooth node** you can alter the steepness of the two curves individually, but you have to alter the direction of both

- with a **symmetrical node** you can only alter the steepness and the direction of both curves by the same amount.

When you draw your curve, CD! determines where the nodes should go and what type they should be, but this does not mean that once it creates, for example, a symmetrical node, you are stuck with it. You can change the type of node quite easily. In fact you can 'edit' nodes in several ways as we shall see, but first things first.

More often than not when you want to adjust a node it will be because you want to move it (and the line associated with it), so let us look at that before we go on to editing nodes.

Adjusting Shapes:
The Shaping tool,
moving curve nodes

1 Begin by making a freehand drawing of a complex curve like this one.

2 Select the Shaping tool and **CLICK** on the curve to get a result like this.

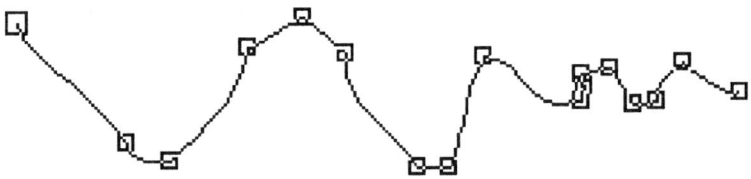

Let us say we want to move the end node. All you have to do is grab, say, the left hand end node, and simply move it to a new position.

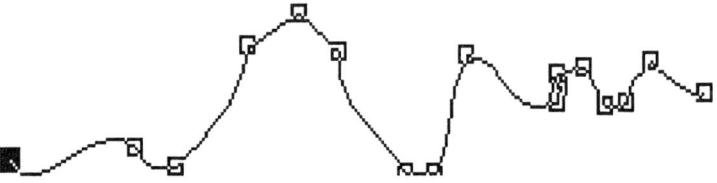

You can do exactly the same with any of the nodes, to alter the shape in any way you want. The curve in the next illustration is the same one as on this page, but you can see we have altered it radically, simply by moving a few nodes individually.

Adjusting Shapes: The Shaping tool, moving curve nodes

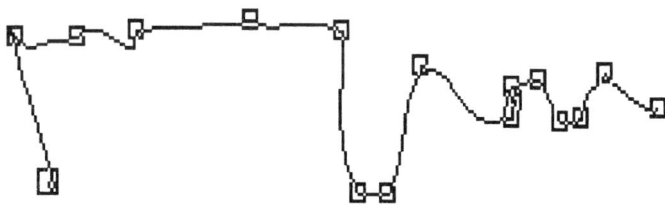

If you select more than one node at a time – either by marquee selecting them, or by holding down SHIFT and then clicking on each in turn (known as **'Shift clicking'**),

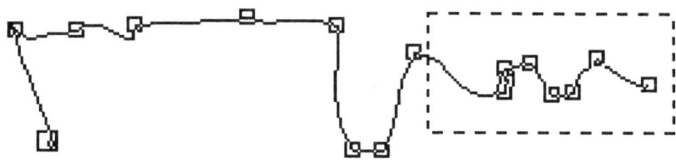

you can move a whole section of the curve, without altering the shape of the bit you are moving.

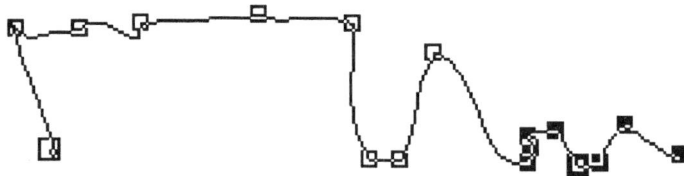

So moving nodes is easy and it can produce good results. By the way, to repeat what we said just now, this curve is still the same one we drew for the illustration at the top of the previous page. All we have done is alter the shape by moving some nodes. Let us now move on to looking at how to edit the nodes themselves.

Adjusting Shapes:
The Shaping tool,
editing curve nodes

1   Begin this exercise by drawing a curve like the above, in freehand mode.

2   Select the **Shaping tool**, choose a node and **DOUBLE CLICK** on it. You will get the node editing menu.

In this illustration we double clicked on the second node on the curve. Notice that the editing menu appears just to the right of the node. Also notice that the segment of the curve which precedes the node is now emboldened (contrast it with the segment of the curve you can see just above the menu). You can also just see some control handles in the picture. They are associated with the first and second nodes on the curve.

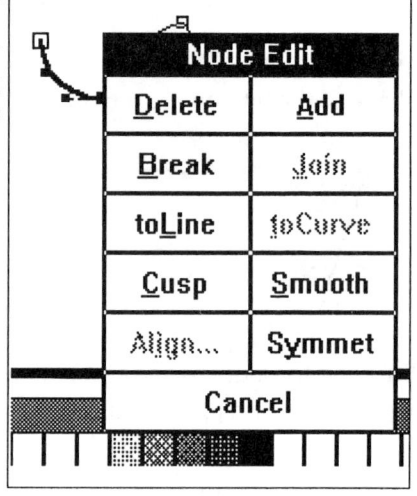

Fig. 3-13 **Node editing menu.**

You can see the situation more clearly if we zoom-in on the curve.

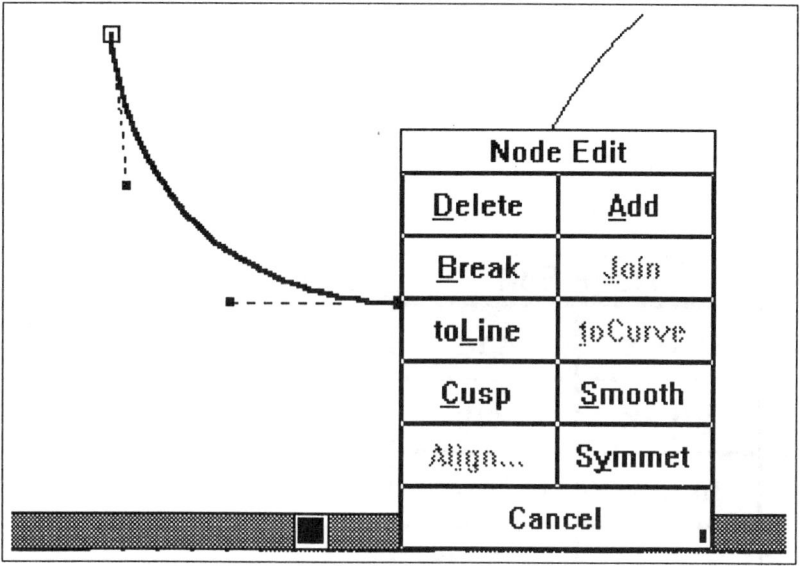

Fig. 3-14 **Zooming in on the previous figure.**

We drew our line from left to right on the screen, which tells you the node we selected was at the end of the segment CD! highlighted. Apart from when you select the first (i.e. the biggest) node in a curve, CD! always highlights the curve segment which precedes it.

You can get the same effect as in Figures 3-13 and 3-14 by double clicking on a curve segment itself. So if you wanted to select, for example, the fourth node in the curve (for editing) you would double click on the third segment of the curve.

Adjusting Shapes:
The Shaping tool,
editing curve nodes

This last point is particularly significant for one of the options at the very top of the Node Editing menu. If you want to Add a new node to the curve, you would double click on the curve, where you want the node to appear. When the menu appears, you will notice that its top left corner will be on the point where you double clicked. When you select the Add option, CD! will generate the node and put it where you indicated.

Node Edit	
Delete	**Add**
Break	**Join**
toLine	**toCurve**
Cusp	**Smooth**
Align...	**Symmet**
Cancel	

Where most of the other options on the menu are concerned, when you double click on a segment and then select an option from the menu, CD! will make changes to the node at the end of the segment.

For two of the buttons on the menu – Align and Join – you need to select two nodes before the options become available, even so, we shall examine all the options on the menu to see what they are for.

Delete is easy to understand. But, remember that CD! generates a node for each change of direction in the curve, so when you delete a node, CD! might alter the shape of the curve quite significantly.

Adjusting Shapes:
The Shaping tool,
editing curve nodes

Add, we have already examined.

Break enables you to make a break in the line at the node you have selected. It means that CD! will generate two nodes where there was one before – one at the end of one object and the other at the beginning of the second object. Then you simply move them apart to see what looks like two objects. In fact CD! still treats them as one.

Join enables you to connect up the two ends of the same curve, or the ends of curves which you have broken apart and it even enables you to join the ends of separate objects, except there is a bit of a complication with this last action. You cannot select two nodes which are on different objects, so before you can join up two separate objects you have to make them into a single object. You do this by selecting the objects with the Pick tool and then tapping Ctrl+C to 'combine' them into one.

Then you can switch back to the Shaping tool and select the two **end** nodes you want to join up. When you double click on one of the nodes, the Node editing menu will appear. By the way, you do not have to superimpose the nodes you want to join. They can be some distance apart; CD! can handle it.

to Line seems like an odd command to have on a 'curve node editing menu' (not only because it starts with a lower case letter).

Adjusting Shapes:
The Shaping tool,
editing curve nodes

So far we have been talking about there being only three types of node, which is true for curves. But, of course, you can draw straight lines and they have to have control nodes at each end, so it follows there must be such a thing as a 'Line node'. A line node does not have to be at the end of a line. It can be positioned somewhere along the length of a path, but it is typified by having a straight line entering it. A line node has a single control handle which means it behaves differently from a curve node. The control handles on a curve node allow you to change the angle and the height of the curve entering and leaving the node, but the control handle on a line node allows you to control only one side of the node (because it sits at the end of a perfectly straight line segment which, by definition, has to remain straight). You can, however move a line node, to lengthen or shorten, or change the slope of the straight line segment.

to Curve enables you to convert a line node into a curve node. 'Nuff said', we think.

Cusp, Smooth and **Symmet** you will recognise as being the different kinds of curve nodes. When you double click on a curve node, or its associated segment of the curve, you will be electing to edit a node which is already one of the three types of curve node. The edit menu enables you to change the node to another type, and so gives you the extra control over the basic shape of the curve about the node point.

Align is the only option on the menu which has a sub-menu, or dialog box. CD! needs to know how you want things aligned.

Adjusting Shapes:
The Shaping tool,
editing curve nodes

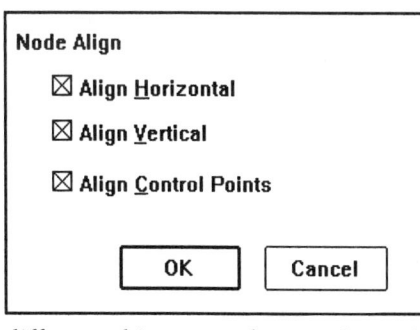

This option works like the Join option we have already examined. You begin by nominating the two nodes you want to align with each other. Here too, they have to be on the same object, so if you want to align nodes which are actually on different objects, you have to begin by combining the objects into one as you do for the Join option. Then you double click on one of the nodes you have selected, select Align from the menu and you will get the dialog box you can see above.

As you can see, the dialog box enables you to specify whether the nodes should be aligned vertically or horizontally, or both. If you select 'both', you can also specify whether their control points should be aligned or not.

Just like other 'Windows' dialog boxes, a cross in one of the little square boxes tells you that the option is selected. To de-select it, simply click on the box to get rid of the cross.

Incidentally the nodes you decide to align do not have to be adjacent to each other.

Adjusting Shapes:
The Shaping tool,
editing curves

We have covered a lot of different points in the last couple of sections, which just goes to show how much control CD! gives you over curves.

By now you will know there are lots of controls but none of them is difficult to use, once you understand how CD! 'thinks'. The upshot is that you have almost infinite command of the images you create. But because the options are so numerous it takes time to really get the hang of things.

So, as we keep saying, take some time to play about with the controls we have been exploring. But don't do it in a haphazard way. Set yourself a specific task – for example, to draw the outline of a car, or a cottage loaf, or a human face. That way you will be able to fine tune your own skills and you will get a better feel for the processes involved.

And don't forget we still have some more shaping controls to examine – starting with those for text. And these are at least as interesting as the ones we have seen so far.

Adjusting Shapes: The Shaping tool, shaping text

If we are going to look at shaping text, we had better get some text on the screen, So:

1   Clear your work page and then key-in, as **string text** (i.e. directly on the page), **Ying Yang for** and tap the **RETURN** key. Then key-in: **Young Blood.**

2   Now select the **Toronto** typeface from the list, set the **point size** to **72**, the **style** to **normal** and check that the **left justification** button is highlighted. Then **CLICK** on **OK**.

3   Move the pointer down to the **red** tablet in the palette and **CLICK** to select this colour for the fill. Open up the pen nib Outlines menu and **CLICK** on the '**X**' to eliminate the outline for the letters. Now get a full page preview (i.e. move the pointer onto the work page and tap the **RIGHT mouse button**).

If you look carefully at the words on screen you will see that the spacing between the 'Ys' and the letters that follow them looks a bit odd. This is quite common in many typefaces and with several letter combinations – for example, with Vo and Ty in the Helvetica face you have the same problem. Also notice that the second line of our text on screen looks untidy because it is shorter than the top line. We can fix these shortcomings with the Shaping tool ... and we can also generate some nice effects.

Adjusting Shapes:
The Shaping tool,
shaping text

The amendments we shall be making also apply to paragraph text, so let us get some paragraph text on screen as well.

1 Get back to your work page. Select the **Text tool** and draw out a bounding rectangle below the string text we already have on screen, of about the same area as that taken up by the string text.

2 The settings will be the same as for our string text, so just as before key-in: **Ying Yang for** and tap the **RETURN** key. Then key-in: **Young Blood** and **CLICK** on **OK**.

3 Move the pointer down to the **blue** tablet in the palette and **CLICK** to select it for the fill. Again as before, open up the pen nib Outlines menu and **CLICK** on the '**X**' to eliminate the outline for the letters. Now get a full page preview (i.e. move the pointer onto the work page and tap the **RIGHT mouse button**).

The letter combinations still look funny. But if you go back to the work page and look at the letter combinations in the paragraph text, you will see they look even worse! There we also have a problem with the 'Blood' combination. Still, it is the look of the preview which matters most.

Adjusting Shapes:
The Shaping tool,
shaping text

1 Select the **Shaping tool** and CLICK on the outline of the **string text**. You will get a result like the one in the left illustration below. Now CLICK on the **bounding box** of the paragraph text and you will get the result on the right.

.Ying .Yang .for   Y.ing .Y.ang .fo.r
.Y.oung .Blood   Y.o.un.g .B.lo.o.d

Notice each character in the text has a node at its bottom left corner and below both types of text there are two stripy arrows; the right hand one pointing right and the left hand one pointing down. These arrows do the same job on both types of text ... but with different results. Let us concentrate on string text for the moment.

1 With the **Shaping tool** selected, CLICK on the outline of the **string text**. Move the screen pointer to the **right facing stripy arrow**, below the text. When you are on it, you will see the pointer change into a cross shape. CLICK AND HOLD to get this (we have omitted the arrow pointer from the illustration):

Adjusting Shapes:
The Shaping tool,
shaping text

2 Now drag the arrow to the right hand side of the page and **RELEASE** to get this result.

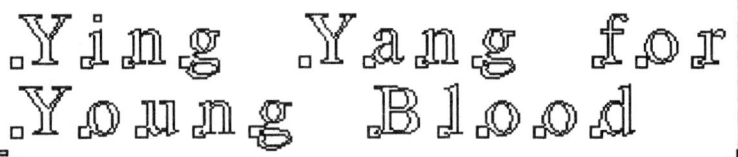

So, pulling the arrow to the right increases the space between the characters in the text. It follows that if you pull the arrow to the left, it decreases the character spacing; compressing the text.

3 Compress the text back to its previous setting by moving the same arrow to the left until the side of the blue outline lines up with the bounding box of the paragraph text.

4 Next, hold down the **Ctrl** key, grab the right hand stripy arrow again and pull out to the right hand side of the page and **RELEASE** to get this end result. Contrast this with the illustration at the top of this page.

Adjusting Shapes: The Shaping tool, shaping text

Even though the scale of the two pictures on the previous page is slightly different, you can see that in the top one it is the space between letters that has changed, while in the lower one the space between words has increased. We still haven't managed to do anything about our funny letter combinations, but we shall get to that shortly. So, pulling the arrow to the right or left, increases or decreases the space between letters and pulling the arrow with Ctrl held down increases or decreases the space between words. How about the space between lines? That is what the other arrow is for.

1   Grab the **left stripy arrow** and pull downwards, then release to get a result something like this.

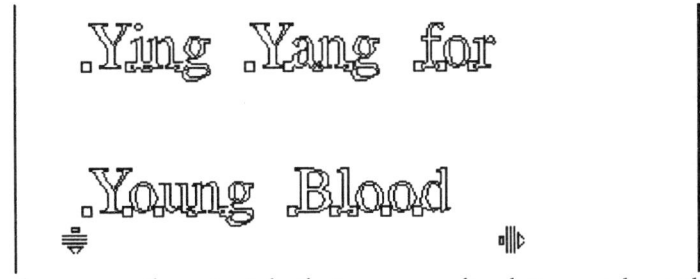

Now we have seen the principle that you can alter letters and words and spaces en-bloc, we can begin to see how we can deal with those funny letter combinations. The answer is to move letters individually. And this is just as easy to do.

1   Begin by zooming-in on the word **Young**.

Adjusting Shapes:
The Shaping tool,
shaping text

At this magnification it is easy to see that there seems to be a much bigger space between the **Y** and the **o** than between the other letters. In fact the spacing is right, it just looks wrong. To make it look right, we need to move the **o** to the left a little (in the jargon, we need to adjust the 'kerning' of the letters). Remember all the letters in both kinds of text have a control node at their bottom left corner.

1   Grab the control node for the **o** and pull it gently to the left.

You will see a dashed outline of the letter move with the pointer. In this illustration you can see this, and you can also see a potential problem. You can move the letter in any direction, which means it is very easy to stray from the 'baseline' of the text. We have exaggerated the problem here, to show the effect.

Luckily the problem is easy to overcome. You just use the 'constrain' key to constrain the letter to the nearest baseline, which in this case is the same baseline as the other letters.

2   Hold down the **Ctrl** key and move the letter back to the baseline. Tuck the letter **o** just under the letter **Y** and then **RELEASE** the click to see another problem.

Adjusting Shapes:
The Shaping tool,
shaping text

Having moved one letter, we have stranded the others in the word. We shall have to move all the other letters over as well. Now to do this individually would be a chore, but, remembering how CD! works, if we select the nodes of all the remaining letters we should be able to move them all across in one go. (In fact, we should have done this when we shifted the **o** across, but we thought we would try to catch you out.)

1   Select all the other nodes in the word (either with a marquee or by shift-clicking on each one in turn). Then hold down **Ctrl** and move them across to make the spacing look right again.

2   Zoom out to the whole work page again and then get a full page preview of your work. **Compare** the **red Young** with the **blue** unaltered **Young.**

A bit more jargon now; the processes you have been looking at are known as 'dynamic' or 'interactive' modifications – you interact with the controls and the image to make things look right.

Adjusting Shapes:
The Shaping tool,
shaping text

Occasionally you have to be more precise about lining things up and you do this by setting the 'attributes' for a character or a group of characters (depending on how many you have selected for processing).

1　Get back to your work page and **Double CLICK** on the node for the letter **Y**.

After a few moments, CD! presents you with this, Character Attributes dialog box.

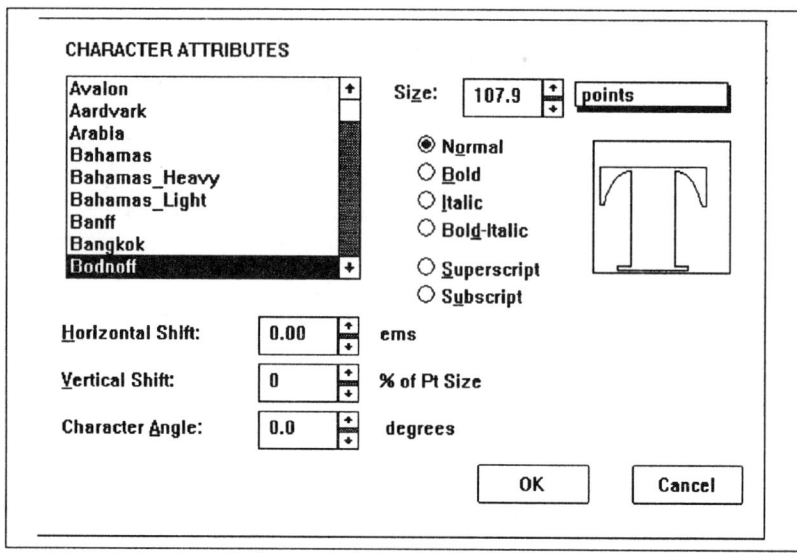

Fig. 3-15　**Setting precise attributes for individual characters.**

Adjusting Shapes: The Shaping tool, shaping text

We know how to use dialog boxes, so we shall simply make some adjustments here. Notice that the current settings for the text (all the text we have created) are echoed here.

1 Increase the **point size** to **108**. Adjust the **horizontal shift** down **to -2 ems.** An 'em' is a rectangle of space equal to that taken up by a capital letter M of a given point size. The minus sign moves the character to the left (+ = right).

We could make several other adjustments, for example, we might choose to shift the character up or down vertically and we could even change the angle of the letter, but you can experiment with these other settings on your own.

2 For now, we shall limit ourselves to the adjustments we have made. Tap **RETURN** to get back to the work page to see a rather peculiar result.

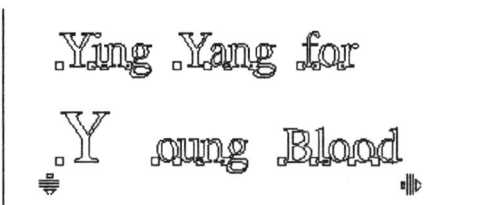

If you think back to when we created this text, you will remember we set it to be left justified – in other words, the leftmost character in the string was to line up with the text crosshair centre line.

Adjusting Shapes:
The Shaping tool,
shaping text

The text in our illustration is lined up at the left hand side – i.e. it is left justified. So, the first character in the second line cannot actually move left, because we told it not to when we created the text in the first place. Therefore, CD! has to fulfil our instruction by moving all the other characters on the line to the right. If we definitely want the character offset to the left, then we have to edit the text and modify the justification setting.

1 Tap the **SPACEBAR**, then tap **Ctrl+T** to get the **Text entry dialog box**. Tap the letter **N** or **CLICK** on the little radio button marked **None** so no justification is set. (Oh, that's why it's there!) Then **CLICK** on **OK** and tap the **SPACEBAR**.

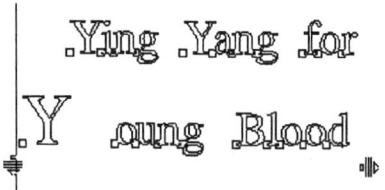

Now the character has shifted to the left by the amount we specified.

In all these examples we have been looking at how string text responds to alteration. The Shape tool gives you pretty much the same controls for paragraph text, but with one major difference, you alter the text, but not the bounding box. You need to remember this, particularly when you are adjusting character and word spacing.

Adjusting Shapes: The Shaping tool, cropping bitmaps

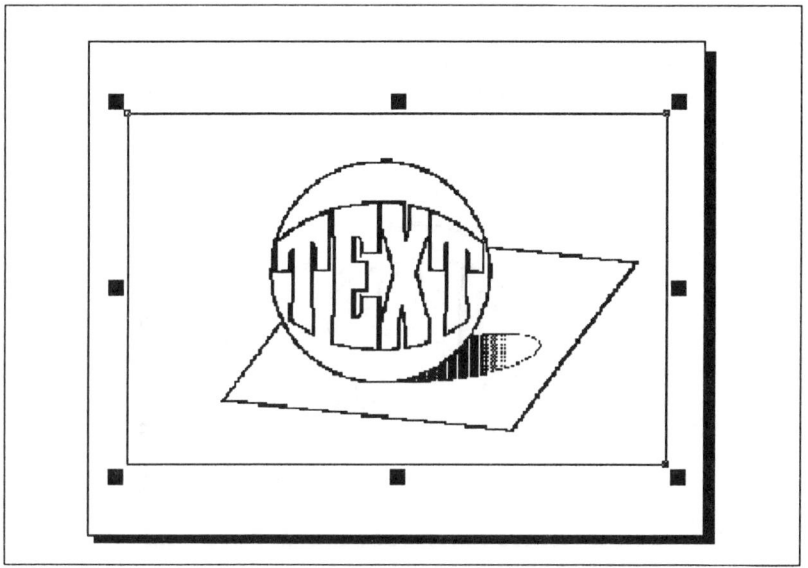

Fig. 3-16 **Textball.pcx - a bitmap of a bitmap in CD!.**

When you import a bitmap image into CD! it comes up as a grey image on the page. In this illustration it looks a lot darker than it does in real life. We imported textball.pcx (a Windows Paintbrush file) with the Shaping tool selected and it appeared with the sizing handles in place.

The handles here work just like the Pick tool sizing handles, in that you grab them to move the sides of the bounding rectangle. The difference with this procedure is that the picture does not change in size as you move the boundary.

Adjusting Shapes:
The Shaping tool,
cropping bitmaps

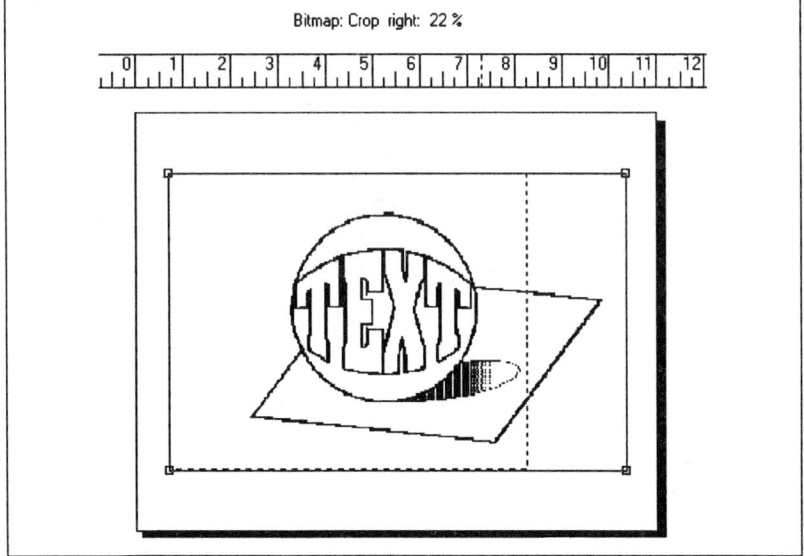

Fig. 3-17 **Cropping the bitmap.**

As you move the sizing handles inwards toward the centre of the picture, you can see less and less of the image. Figure 3-17 shows what happens when you start to move the right hand edge of the bounding rectangle inwards. Notice the dashed ghost line and the status line message.

You repeat the exercise on the other sides of the bounding rectangle until you end up with only the image you want. Then you can check how it will look on the page by getting a full page preview. If necessary you can adjust outwards again if you have cropped too much.

Adjusting Shapes:
The Shaping tool,
cropping bitmaps

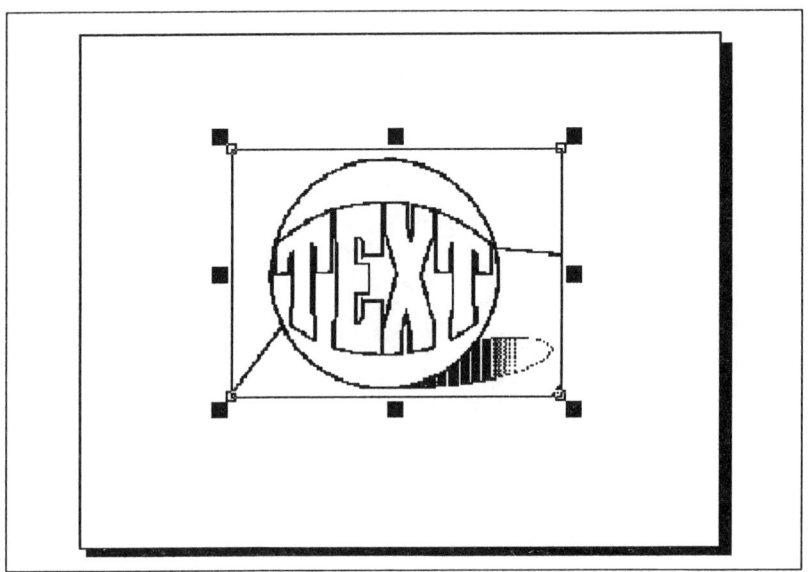

Fig. 3-18 **Cropping - the final image on the work page.**

If you want to use part of a bitmapped image, but you want to distort the image to get a specific effect, then you will have to go about the process in a particular way. CD! cannot crop a bitmap which has been rotated or skewed. So you will have to import the image, then crop it with the Shaping tool and only then switch to the Pick tool to rotate or skew the cropped picture.

When you rotate or skew the bitmap CD! blanks it out and puts a white triangle in what was the bottom left corner of the image so you can tell which way up it is.

Adjusting Shapes:
The Shaping tool,
rotate and skew bitmaps

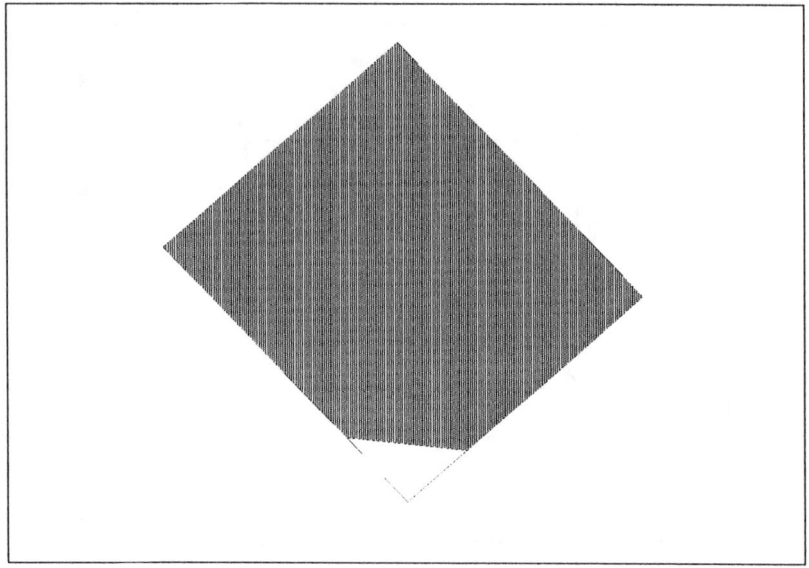

Fig. 3-19 **A cropped and rotated bitmap.** (The striped effect is a function of the printing processes for this book.)

There will be times when cropping and rotating or skewing a bitmap will not give you the precise effect you want. If you are importing a scanned image, or one created in, say, Windows Paintbrush, you could try doctoring the image before you import it into CD!. But, if this is not possible, you still have another option open to you, you can tell CD! to import it for tracing. When you trace the object, CD! will create an image in its own 'vector graphics' format which you can then modify, stretch, scale, rotate, skew, etc. at will, without reducing the quality of the final result on the printed page.

Autotracing bitmaps

If you want to import a very complex graphic and you don't particularly want to get involved in the process, then you should probably use the CorelTRACE program which came with CD!. On many occasions, though, CD!'s built-in AutoTrace feature will give you the results you want. Here is how it works. (We have assumed that you already have a .PCX or .PCC file on disc.)

1 Hold down the **Alt** key then tap the letter **F** and the letter **I** to select the **Import** option from the **File** menu.

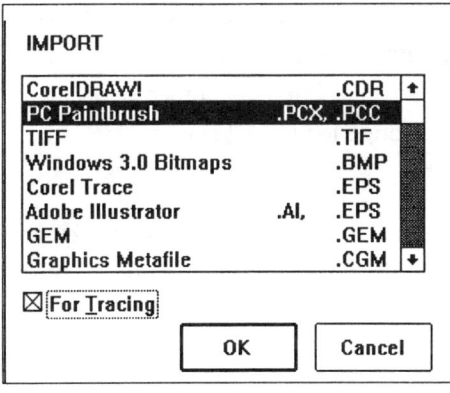

You will get this dialog box. Notice that we have selected **PC Paintbrush .PCX .PCC** from the list of format options in the window.

We have also clicked on the little square (bottom left), labelled **For Tracing**. This last item is critical.

2 When you have set things up properly, CLICK on OK.

You then go through the rest of the Import procedure, which we do not want to describe yet. (If you want to try the procedure now, see the File menu sections in Part Five of this book.)

Autotracing bitmaps

3 With the **Pick tool**, CLICK on the outline of the image to select it for processing (if it isn't already selected). Then select the **Lines and curves** drawing tool.

Your cursor will change to look something like this: —¦—

4 It is best to zoom-in on part of the image. Place the cursor just to the left of a bit you want to trace, CLICK and then wait a few moments for CD! to trace the bit you have selected.

CD! will trace all parts of the image that are contiguous with the small part you have indicated, so on a simple image it may trace the whole lot. Most likely, though, you will have to zoom-in on other parts of the image to ensure the whole thing is converted to CD! curves.

5 When you are sure you have traced all of the image you want to trace, select the **Pick tool**, CLICK on the outline of the original bitmap and tap **Delete** to get rid of it.

6 Select the **Shaping tool** and get on with tidying up the curves and lines CD! has created.

The illustration in Figure 3-20 shows a bitmap we have traced and then selected for shaping. You can see it is not an absolutely precise copy of the bitmap image, but it is close enough for us to replicate it, or completely transform it, if we want to.

Autotracing bitmaps

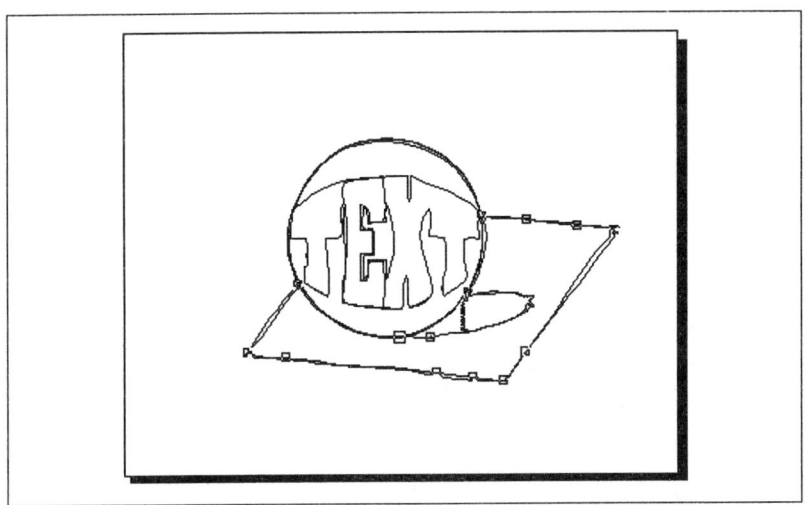

Fig. 3-20 **An AutoTraced image, ready for processing.**

If you want AutoTrace to track the image more closely than it did in our picture you can modify the AutoTrace Tracking setting in the LINES & CURVES preferences dialog box which we have already mentioned on a couple of occasions.

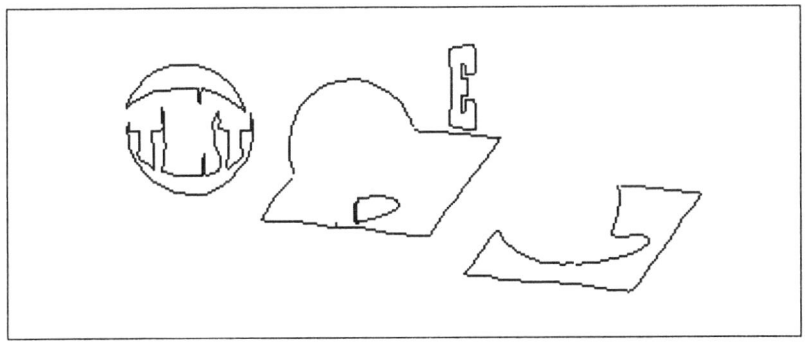

Fig. 3-21 **Now this is a severely modified former bitmap..!**

Adjusting Shapes

The next logical step when we are talking about modifying the images we are creating, is to think about altering the lines and fills of our objects. In fact we have already seen how to do that to an extent – by using the pen nib fly-out menu and the colour palette at the bottom of the screen (left mouse button for fill colour and right button for line colour).

You won't be surprised to know that CD!'s facilities are a great deal more comprehensive than this. But, given the aims of this book and other **Step By Step** books, it would be wrong to go on an excursion down the by-ways of colour processing. There are many books dedicated to the subject of colour processing and colour systems which can give the topic the attention it deserves.

So we have decided to explore the two topics of Lines and Fills without spending too much time on the intricacies of Colour. In the next chapter we shall examine the controls for Line settings and a few of the effects you can generate, then we shall have a look at some of the Fill effects. We shall concentrate on using the various colour facilities open to you, without getting into the underlying theory.

(If you feel you need more information about different colour systems and using colours, you will find a useful introduction to the topic in various places in your CD! User's manual. See also the bibliography in Appendix B to the manual.)

PART FOUR
Line and Fill Settings

Outline attributes

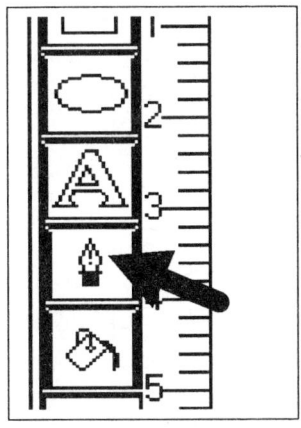

Fig. 4-1 **Outline attributestool.**

You already know that when you click on the 'Outline attributes' pen nib icon, you get the fly-out menu which you can see at the bottom of this page.

Normally you would have opened up this menu when you were working on one of your objects and the options you choose from the menu would apply just to that object. If you open up the menu while no objects are selected and then click on either the Pen nib icon, or the Paintbrush icon you are asked whether the settings you are about to implement from here on should apply to all new objects you create, or just text objects, or just objects other than text.

You make your choice by clicking on the appropriately labelled radio button, or by tapping in the letter **A** for All objects, **T** for Text objects only, or **O** for just objects 'Other' than text. CD! then moves on to a rather large dialog box which offers various options.

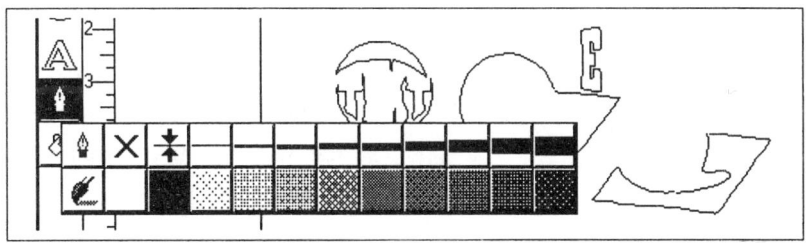

Fig. 4-2 **The Line Attributes 'fly-out' menu of options.**

Outline Attributes:
Pen settings

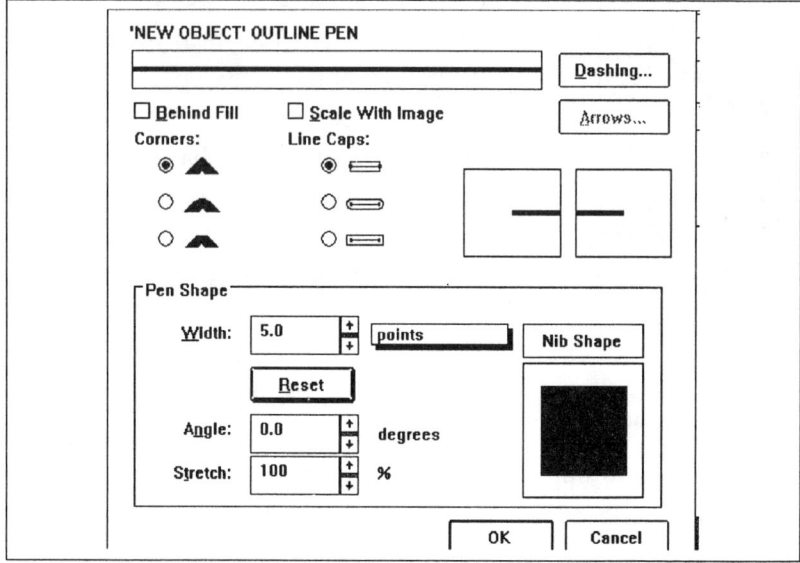

Fig. 4-3 **Outline Pen settings dialog box.**

We don't want to go into too much detail here, you can get that from the User's Manual, but it is worthwhile for us to point out some of the effects you can get. For example, Figure 4-4 shows four changes we have made to the default settings in Figure 4-3. See if you can find them.

Changes like this enable us to create this effect. We produced the word in two parts, with different pen settings. The first part of the word uses settings similar to those in Figure 4-4 (but we have exaggerated them for clarity in this illustration).

Outline Attributes: Pen settings

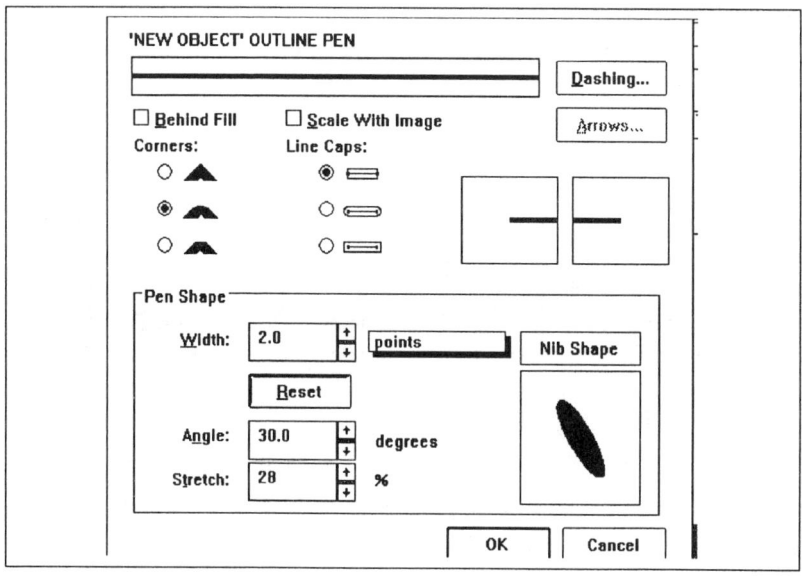

Fig. 4-4 **Outline Pen settings dialog box. Spot the 4 changes.**

Notice in particular that **'Scri'** has lines of varying thickness, while those in **'ptor'** are all of same thickness. We created this result by changing the angle, the nib shape (stretch) and the width of the outline.

As for the rest of the pen settings on the fly-out menu, well you have used them already so we won't add much more other than to draw your attention to Figure 4-5, which provides more detail in a nutshell.

Outline Attributes:
Pen settings

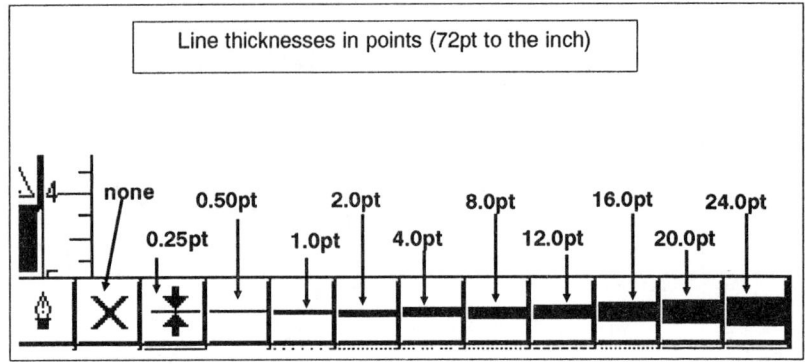

Fig. 4-5 **Line thicknesses.**

If you look back at Figures 4-3 and 4-4 you will see that you can also create dashed lines and you can fix arrowheads to your lines. Both processes are simple and both follow the same general procedure.

You begin by clicking on the relevant button (near the top right of the dialog box). CD! presents you with a further dialog box. On this dialog box you will find a window of sample patterns. You simply scroll through the examples until you see the one you want. You select that one by clicking on it. CD! gives you an instant display of how it looks. When you are selecting arrows, you click the left button for the start arrow head (i.e. where you start the arrow from) and the right button for the finish arrowhead (i.e. the end of the line you drew).

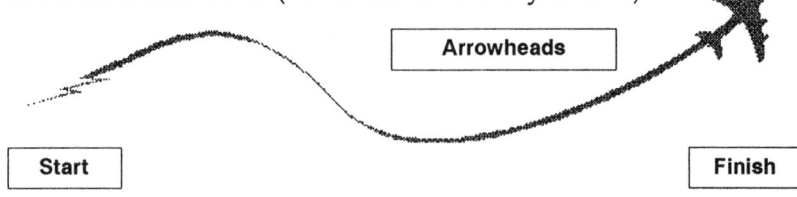

You can also create arrowheads of your own design through the Special menu. If this is a job you will be doing, see your User's Manual for the details.

Meanwhile, back at the Outline Pen dialog box ... There are two other items we need to examine: Behind Fill and Scale With Image.

Behind Fill

This means, put the outline of the object behind the fill for the object. This has more of an effect when the outline is quite wide. like this:

On the left hand side the outline is in front of the white fill, while on the right the outline is 'behind fill' (wherever he is).

Scale With Image

Simply means increase or decrease the width of the outline by the same scale as any increases or decreases in the size of the object. So you get this result:

Here you can see that the ratio of line width to size of letter looks about the same on both text objects.

Outline Attributes:
Grey scales

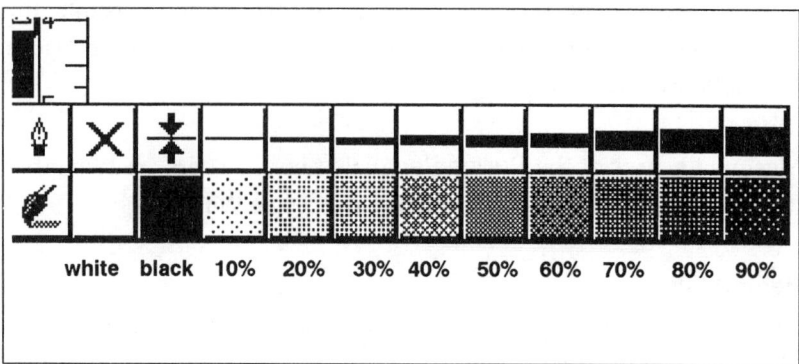

Fig. 4-6 **Line grey scales.**

The fly-out menu provides you with immediate access to various shades of grey for your lines. White is 0% black and black is 100% black and you have nine other shades ranging from 10% to 90% black. Also, if you look at the colour palette at the bottom of the screen (you may have to move it left as far as it will go), you will see that you have the same selection there. Remember, we have already seen that you can select colours (and grey shades) from the screen palette by clicking the left mouse button for the fills and the right mouse button for the lines of a selected object.

The Paintbrush icon at the left hand end of the fly-out menu for outline attributes gives you immediate access to colour settings for lines. We shall not open up this icon now, because we would plunge straightaway into the theory of colour systems. So, instead, we shall move on to look at Fills and the effects you can get with them.

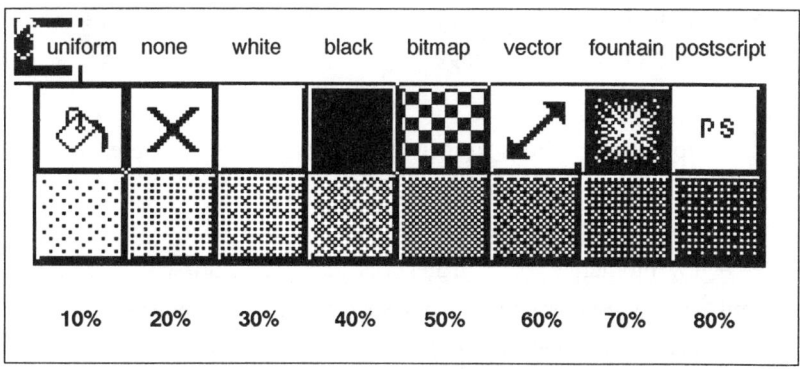

Fig. 4-7 **The 'Fill' fly-out menu - types of fill and grey scales.**

In this section we shall concentrate on fill patterns and textures. We shall be looking at one or two colour items which are immediately available ... and how you use them.

So we shall not be looking at the first type of fill, because when you click on that icon you go straight into handling colour. For the time being, we shall continue to use the screen palette for setting fills of a uniform colour. The next three options will be familiar to you: the **X** means 'no fill', while the white and black icons will give you white and black fills for the selected object(s). The grey scales in the lower section of the fly-out menu will also be familiar, because they work in the same way as the grey scales for lines.

That leaves four interesting options and we shall look at each in turn during the remainder of this part of the book.

Fill Attributes:
Bitmap fills

1   Begin by clearing your work page. Then draw a rectangle which half fills the page.

2   Open up the **Fills fly-out menu** and **CLICK** on the chequered '**Bitmap**' icon.

After a few moments you will get this dialog box on screen. You will recognise some familiar components, such as 5 sample patterns displayed in a row across the lower part of the box. There are 49 such pattern 'tiles' built-in to CD! and, as we shall see, you can create more, either by editing an existing pattern, or by generating a completely new one.

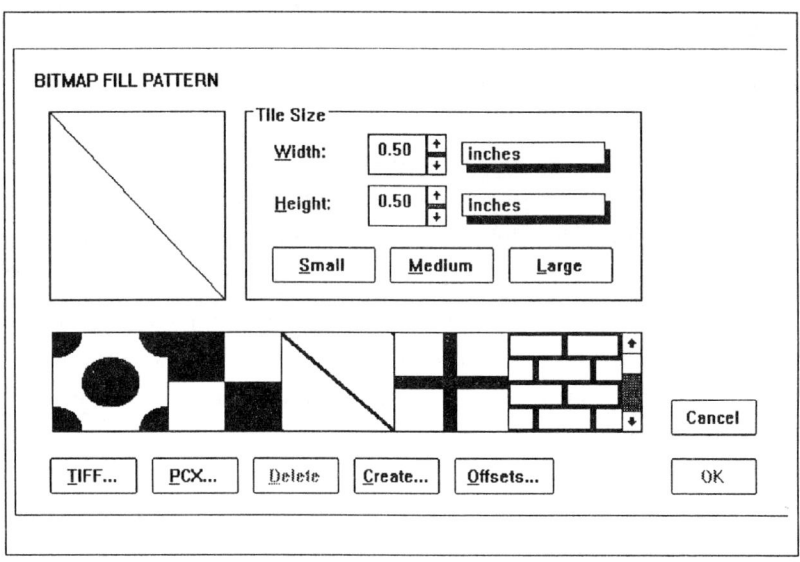

Fig. 4-8   **Selecting a bitmap fill pattern - dialog box.**

Fill Attributes:
Bitmap fills

Alongside the five samples, there are the usual scroll controls to enable you to browse through the available examples.

3 Find one you like and CLICK on it to see how it looks as a pattern.

The preview box at the top left hand corner gives you an immediate impression of the result. If you don't like it, select another.

Perhaps you don't like the pattern because it is the wrong size. That is easy to overcome, because you can set the size of the pattern elements in two ways.

4 You will see three buttons just to the right of the preview box, marked **Small**, **Medium** and **Large**. CLICK on each one in turn and watch the preview box.

You will see the pattern in the preview box change size with each click. You will also see the height and width settings change at the same time. CD! sets the width and the height to be the same but you do not have to stick to the same aspect ration. You may decide that a particular pattern would be just right if it were slightly taller or more squat. So, you can adjust it until it looks right for you.

5 Adjust the pattern you have selected by adjusting the height and width settings and then CLICK on **OK**. Wait for a moment.

Fill Attributes:
Bitmap fills

After a short pause CD! displays its 'BITMAP PATTERN COLOR' (sic) selector screen. This screen has two identical colour palettes, one for the foreground colour (the bits that were in black on the pattern you selected – if you prefer, foreground = outline, at least on most of the patterns) and it has a palette for the background colour, the white bits. You can see only a relatively small section of the full palettes on screen. Notice that both have scroll controls on the right hand side.

6   Make sure that both palettes are scrolled up as far as they will go and make sure that **Process** method is selected. From the **Foreground palette** select the **pure blue** (third from the left in the top row). You will see the name appear in the rectangle at the top of the palette. Now select **pure red** from the **background palette** (fourth from the right in the top row). Have a look at the effect in the preview box. (If you don't like it, select another combination of colours.)

7   Finally, CLICK on OK to get back to the work page. Then get a full page preview. See what you think ... and then get back to the work page and open up the **Fills fly-out menu** again. Select the chequered **bitmap icon** again.

Along the bottom of the dialog box you will see a row of five buttons. **T̲IFF...** and **P̲CX...** enable you to create new bitmap pattern 'tiles' by reading-in an image you created earlier.

Fill Attributes:
Bitmap fills

When you click on either of these buttons (depending on the type of file you want to load), CD! displays a second dialog box. This dialog box is a file selection box, through which you specify the 'path' to the file you want and its name. When you select the file, CD! returns to the first dialog box and proceeds to construct a tile of the new pattern.

After a short pause you get a result like the one in Figure 4-9. Here you can see that we have imported an image created by Windows Paintbrush, but notice the shape of the image in the row of selection boxes and that in the preview box. We have had to stretch the image sideways by 60% to correct a distortion which occurred during loading.

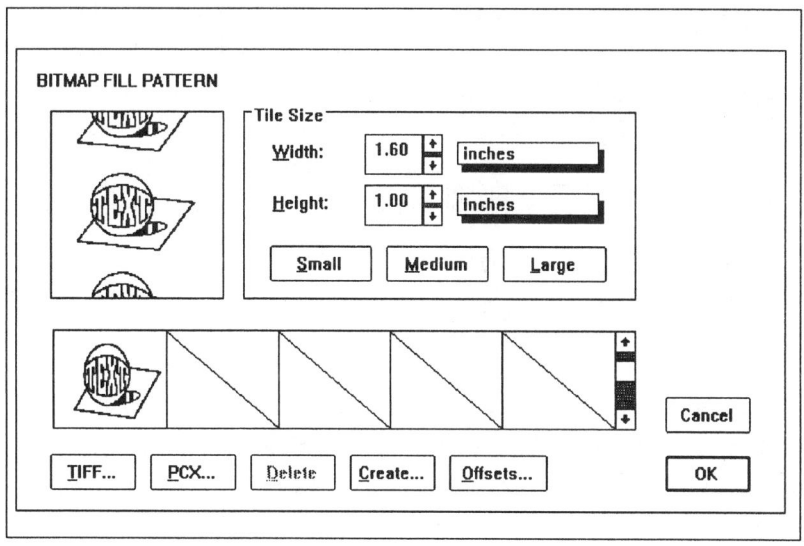

Fig. 4-9 **Importing a new bitmap tile pattern.**

Fill Attributes:
Bitmap fills

Distortions can and do occur during loading, for a number of reasons, which is why CD! gives you control over the final image you use. Notice also that the image in the selector box is in the centre of the tile. If you look at the size of the tile (just to the right of the preview box) you will see it is one inch high. At that scale two images should just fit onto the tile, but we have one image in the middle of the tile and two halves of it at the top and the bottom. This because we clicked on the **Offsets...** button and then specified that the

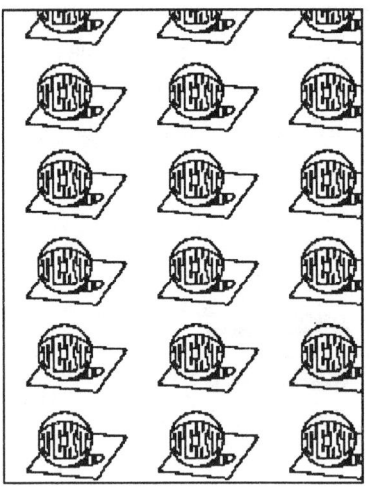

image should be offset by 50% of the tile height (notice: '50% of the **tile** height', not 50% of the image height!). Had we wanted to, we could have offset the image by anything between 1 to 100% of the tile size vertically or horizontally. And, where an image is repeated several times to form rows and columns on the tile, you can offset the rows or the columns by a certain percentage of the tile side. On the left is the final pattern on our rectangle.

The **Create...** button enables you to create a completely new bitmap pattern from scratch, or to edit an existing pattern. When you click on the button, CD! displays its BITMAP PATTERN EDITOR screen, which you can see in Figure 4-10. In this example, we have created a pattern using the coarsest size setting of 16 x 16.

Fill Attributes
Bitmap fills

In Figure 4-10 you can see the editing screen, a matrix of square picture elements (pixels) to the left of the picture, while to the right you have two sets of control settings. Apart from the 16 x 16 screen you can also select a screen of either 32 x 32 picture elements or 64 x 64 elements. You create the pattern by moving the screen pointer onto one of the picture elements on the blank screen and clicking the left mouse button to colour the element black, or the right mouse button to make it white again. You can change the pen size to speed things up a bit, so you can colour either four or eight 'pixels' with each click. When you click on OK, CD! takes you back to the BITMAP FILL PATTERN dialog box and adds the new pattern to the end of the existing library.

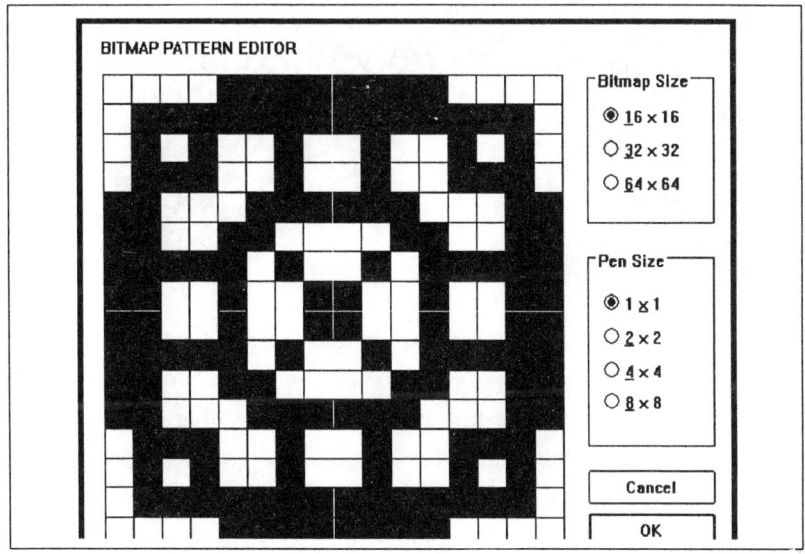

Fig. 4-10 **The Bitmap pattern editor in use.**

Fill Attributes: Bitmap fills

All you have to do then is select the pattern from the library. As you proceed back to the work page (via the colour selection dialog box), CD! automatically fills the selected object with your new bitmap pattern. The outline and fill indicator in the top right of the work screen shows the chequered pattern to tell you that the selected object has a bitmap fill.

You can process such an image in the usual ways, including skewing and rotating, but notice that the bitmap pattern remains unaltered by the transformations, because the object merely acts as a window through which you can see the fill.

We have one action button left on our dialog box, the **Delete** button. You use it by clicking on the sample pattern you want to get rid of and then clicking on the **Delete** button. CD! will check that you really do want to delete the pattern and when you tell it to go ahead it will blank out the sample tile. But the pattern will remain on the selected object! You will need to select another pattern or another type of fill if that is not what you want.

Fill Attributes:
Vector pattern fills

1   Begin by clearing your work page. Then draw a rectangle which half fills the page.

2   Open up the **Fills fly-out menu** and CLICK on the third icon from the right, the double headed arrow, **Vector pattern,** icon.

Your screen will look like the one in Figure 4-11, except the preview box will be empty. You can see that we have already selected a pattern from the range offered by CD! as standard. Clicking on the OK button will take you on to the dialog box illustrated in Figure 4-12.

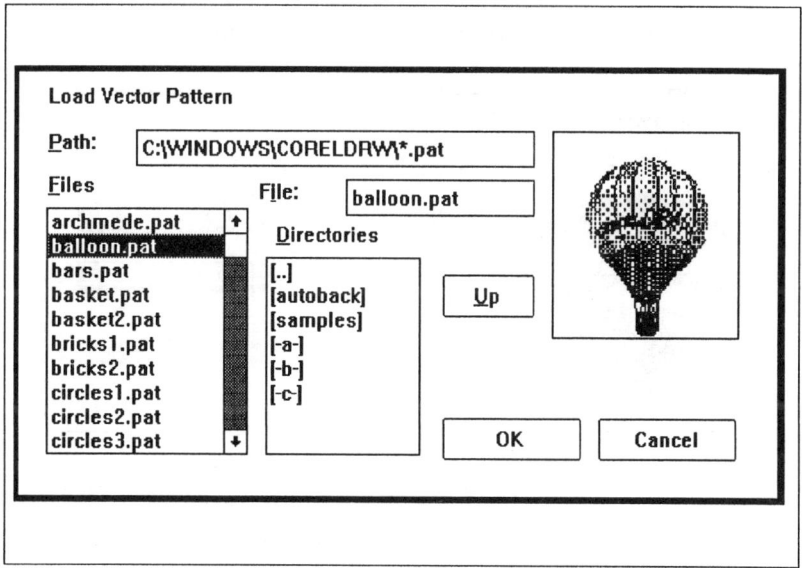

Fig. 4-11 **Selecting a vector pattern from disc.**

Fill Attributes:
Vector pattern fills

You can see from the screen snapshot in Figure 4-12 that modifying a vector pattern involves using the same controls as those you use when modifying bitmap patterns, with one addition: '**Seamless Tiling**'. On some computers a vector pattern tile can have a noticeable seam when several of them are placed to fill an object. This is because the background colour of the pattern is a 'dithered' colour rather than a pure one. In a pure colour, each pixel assumes the same colour, but a dithered colour is one where adjacent pixels are of different colours to give the effect of a mixed colour. On a postscript printer this should not matter, but on other kinds of printer the seams might show. As with bitmap fills, your object is merely a window through which you can see the pattern. If you change the object (i.e. the window) size or shape, the pattern remains unchanged; you will merely see more or less of the pattern.

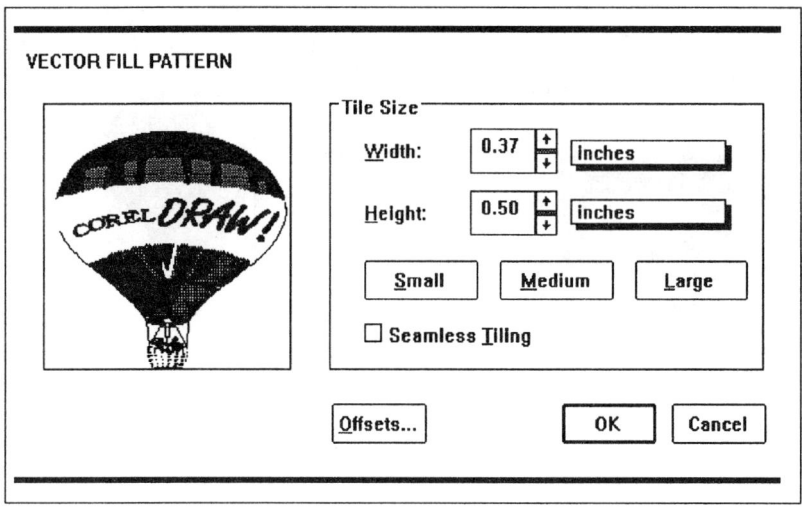

Fig. 4-12 **Specifying a vector pattern.**

Fill Attributes: Fountain fills

1 As before, begin by clearing your work page. But this time, draw a perfect circle which half fills the page.

2 Open up the **Fills fly-out menu** and CLICK on the second icon from the right, the **Fountain fill**, icon.

After a short pause, CD! displays the screen you can see in Figure 4-13. In this screen snapshot the preview box does not show up very well – the real thing is at much higher definition and you can see a gradual merging from 20% black at the bottom of the preview to 100% black at the top. Notice you can see even horizontal bands on this 'linear' Fountain fill.

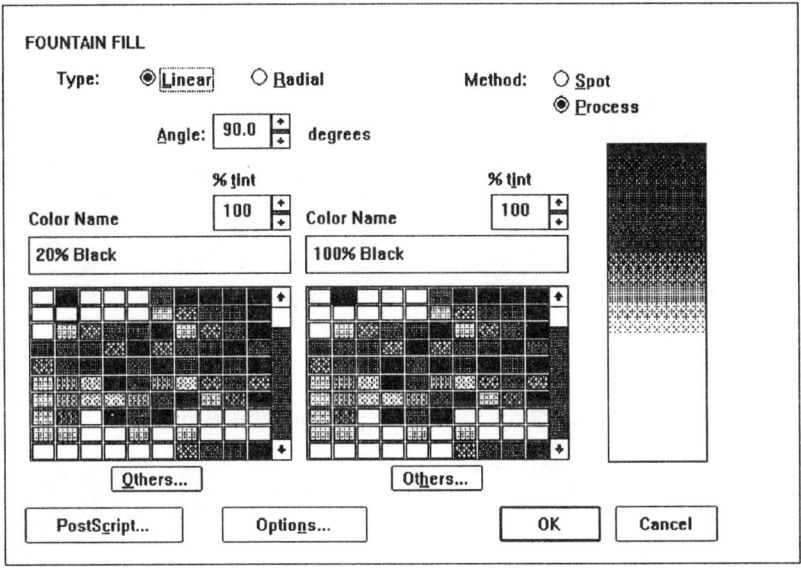

Fig. 4-13 **Specifying a Fountain Fill.**

Fill Attributes:
Fountain fills

If you click on the little radio button labelled **Radial**, you get this effect in the preview box (and on your selected object). (Again, the real image shows a much more gradual merging from one colour to the other, which is very difficult to show in a screen snapshot.)

So a Fountain fill is one where one colour merges gradually into another. Figure 4-13 shows that you have a wide range of colours to choose from – two separate palettes. You can see that, for this example, we chose 20% black as our starting (or inner) colour and we chose 100% black for our ending (or outer) colour. Once you apply the effect to your object, you get results like those below. The three letters on the left are filled with a standard linear fill, those on the right are filled with a standard radial fill.

For this next example we have modified the fills by clicking on the **Options...** button and then making adjustments to the angle of the linear fill and by offsetting the centre point of the radial fill.

This version of LINRAD is exactly the same as the one at the bottom of the previous page, except we have put the outline behind the fill.

In this next example, both words have a centred radial fill, but for the one on the right – via the options button – we increased the 'Edge padding' to 25%. This has the effect of increasing the amount of the starting colour (in this case white) which appears on the object.

The visual effect is to shift the merging start point, away from the very edge of the object. Indeed, with circles or complex shapes, the merging start point may actually be outside the figure. This comes about because CD! fountain fills the notional rectangle which surrounds the object, not the object itself. As with vector and bitmap fills, the shape of the object is a window through which you can see the pattern.

There are three buttons on the Fountain Fill dialog box which we have not examined. Two of them, labelled **Others...**, enable you to choose other colours. The one labelled **Postscript...** enables you to modify the halftone screens printed by a postscript printer, and so get different effects when you print your image. (See the CD! User's Manual pp162 and 163.)

Fill Attributes: Postscript fills

If you have access to a postscript printer, then the last (rightmost) item on the Fills fly-out menu will be of interest as well. Through this option you can fill your objects with a wide range of postscript patterns – you will find the full library of patterns in Appendix A of the CD! User's Manual.

1 Get some string text on your work page and then open up the **Fills fly-out menu. CLICK** on the **PS** icon at the right hand end of the menu.

After a short pause you will get the Postscript Texture dialog box.

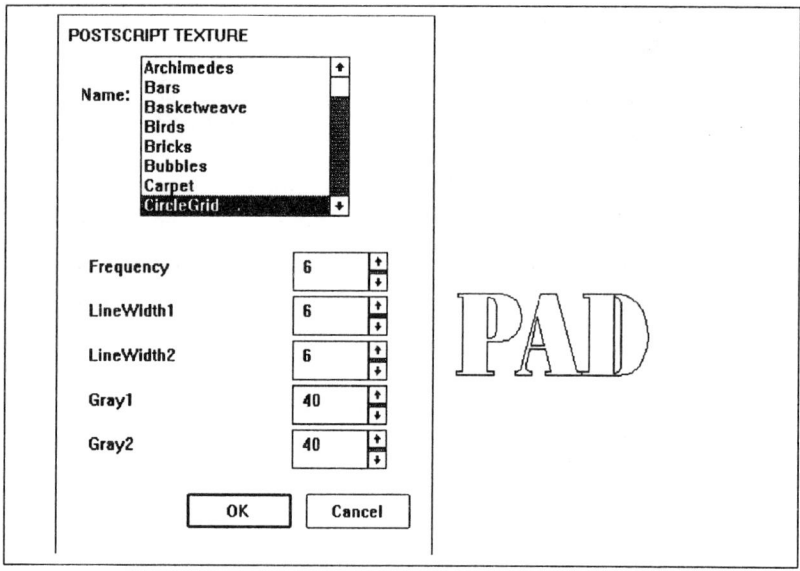

Fig. 4-14 **Selecting a Postscript Texture.**

You make your selection from this dialog box by scrolling the list of available textures until you can see the name of the one you want. Then you simply click on it in the normal way. The set of 5 parameters for textures changes to a basic setting determined by CD!. Different textures have different basic settings, but you can modify these settings to suit yourself. Bear in mind, though, that some of the textures are very detailed and complex and they will take a long time to print. The parameters use a range of measurement systems: 'Frequency' refers to the number per inch, 'Line width' are measured in so many thousandths of an inch and the 'Gray' settings are percentages of black (with 100% grey equating to black and 0% grey equating to white).

When you have made your selection you click on OK as usual. Back at the work page you will see the name of the fill texture you have chosen. It appears next to the Line and Fill indicator box in the top right hand corner of the screen. The indicator box itself will not be filled with the pattern. Instead, you will see the letters PS filling the box. When you get a full page preview you will see that CD! also fills the outline with PS, rather than giving you a preview of the postscript texture on screen. You will have to print-off a copy of the image to see the end result.

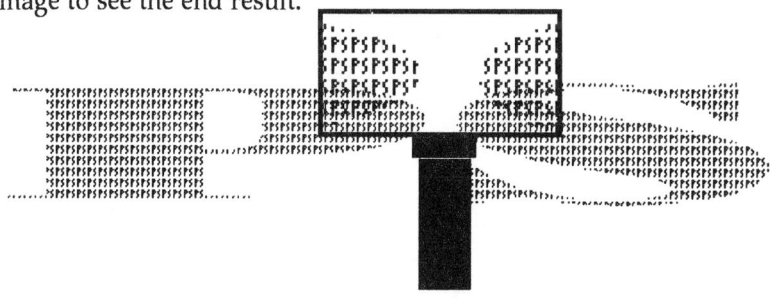

PART FIVE
About Menus

CD! and DOS and Windows

If you have used other 'applications' with Microsoft Windows, you will know that they and CD! have many similarities. This comes about simply because they are running in the Windows environment. Windows is a program which, as it were, interposes itself between the computer's own 'operating system' and the particular software programs you use and this fact alone has implications for the way you work the computer.

Now, if these words mean very little to you, be thankful you're not suffering from technospeak and relax because we shall now say what we mean ... in English, (though you may like to look at the Glossary as well).

When you switch on your computer it is brain dead. It has lots of little bits all buzzing with vitality and raring to go. But go where? And do what? The various bits don't know. They are unco-ordinated and, therefore, useless. They have to be told what to do and when – even to perform simple functions, like sending a signal between the computer and the monitor, so something appears on the screen. The thing that manages the way the computer bits work in a co-ordinated way, is a software program known as an 'Operating System' – so called because it manages the computer system's operation. But operating systems have historically been written by terribly clever people who knew all about those banks of little black shiny bits hidden in the guts of the designer boxes. So, they wrote software which would make it easy for them to control and command these new-fangled personal computer things. But what was easy for them, was not necessarily easy for people like us and that led to a problem.

CD! and DOS and Windows

It meant that normal people – who wanted to drive the things, rather than tinker about – were forced to interact with their computers via the keyboard. And they had to key-in lengthy and arcane incantations such as, 'MAKEDIR C: \WINDOWS\CORELDRW\SAMPLES' as just one example. What's worse, you had to remember all the magic spells and you had to know what they meant. But even more fundamentally, you had to have an idea of how computers worked and how they were organised – otherwise how would you know which spell to use and when to use it? (And don't forget that for many people, the spells were in a foreign language: American.)

Then someone had a bright idea! Why ask people to send memos to their computers ... why not use sign language instead? Why not make the computer (to quote the hateful lie) 'User Friendly'? And they set about designing software that would manage the working environment for the user. Hence we now have Environment Managers such as GEM and Windows. But, remember that programs such as these, are themselves a kind of computer application!

Computers still have operating systems (yours is probably called PCDOS or MSDOS or DRDOS – or just DOS for short) and you still have to interact with it from time to time if you want to get the very best out of your computer. But it might well be that your computer has been set up, so you don't even see DOS, except for a few seconds while you are closing down at the end of your working session.

CD! and DOS
and Windows

Even so, you need to be aware that when the computer does things for you, it is the DOS operating system that makes things happen. So, while you might choose not to use DOS, you will still need to know a bit about how the computer does things before you can really understand how to get the best from Windows.

So, to over-simplify a little, we end up with a situation where, when you start-up your computer, it automatically loads DOS, which provides the right 'environment' for the computer and its software to work. Then it (or you) loads Windows, which runs in the DOS environment. You then interact with Windows to do the things you want to do (e.g. load and run CD!) and Windows interprets your sign language and passes on the appropriate instructions to DOS for it to implement.

There is no doubt that Windows does some wonderful things and it makes the actual operation of the computer very easy ... provided you know what you are doing. One end result of using the Windows environment manager is that all the application programs which run in it have similarities, just because they are running in Windows and because they use some of Window's facilities (like the printing procedures, for example). So it is worthwhile getting familiar with Windows. For our part, we shall be pointing out some of the Windows characteristics you will meet in CD! but if you want a comprehensive treatment of the topic of Windows, see:

Step By Step 'Using Windows 3' by Arthur Tennick
(ISBN No: 0 7506 0080 2)

Selecting a menu

Along the top of your screen, between the CD! window title bar and CD!'s status area, you have a selection of menus, from File through to Special. Each of these menus contains a selection of options which you can choose. The idea of a menu is that a wide range of tasks (more than 70) can be organised into logically similar groupings. So, for example, all the activities concerned with moving information from and to disc are grouped under the File menu heading. Some of the menus are concerned with the objects you are creating, some are to do with setting up CD! for your system.

We shall start with the Effects menu, partly because we have been discussing effects so far, but mostly because it opens up activities which are both impressive and enjoyable.

You can get access to the options on this menu, like all Windows (and therefore, CD!) menus, in several ways:

1 Start by creating, as string text, the word **TEXT**, in the **Aardvark** typeface in **72pt**. Place it in the top right hand quadrant of the page and give it a pure red fill. We can now open the menu, using any one of three methods. You might like to try them. (To cancel the menu, tap the **Esc** key.)

2 Method 1: CLICK on the name of the menu.
Method 2: Tap the **Alt** key (you may need to do it twice) and then tap the letter **C** (notice it is underlined in the menu name).
Method 3: Hold down the **Alt** key and then tap the letter **C**.

Selecting an option from a menu

You will see a flag menu drop down from the menu bar. Don't do anything else for the moment, while we take a look at the components of a typical menu (see Figure 5-1).

The first thing to notice is, some of the items are in grey lettering. As on the dialog boxes you have seen so far, items which appear in grey lettering are not available to you at the moment. This may be for a number of reasons, e.g. perhaps you have not selected an object for processing (in the case of 'Blend', near the bottom of the menu you need to select two objects before it becomes available).

The Edit Envelope option is in reverse video, which means if you tap RETURN, or CLICK on it, that option will be selected for you.

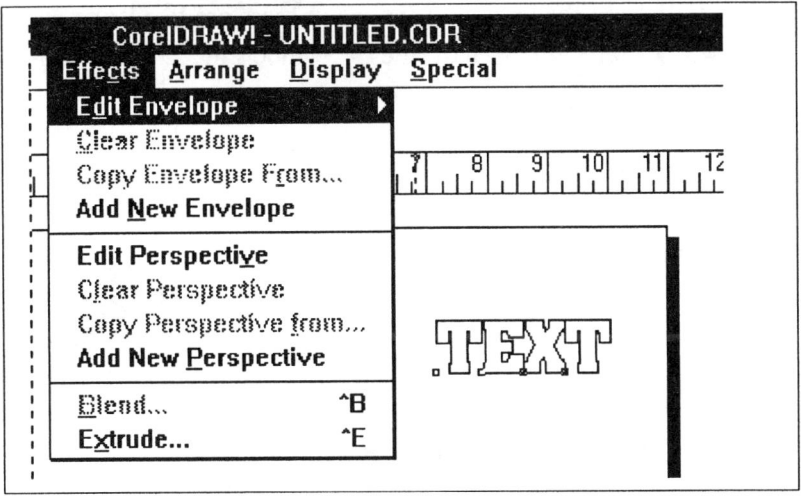

Fig. 5-1   **The Effects menu.**

Selecting an option from a menu

Before we do that, notice that at the right hand end of the highlighted line there is an arrowhead pointing to the right. This tells you there is a further menu for this option.

3   Tap **RETURN**.

Another menu of four options appears to the right of the menu, as you can see in this illustration.

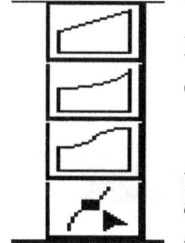

We shall come Back to this sub-menu in a short while. For the moment let us continue with our exploration of a typical CD! (and Windows) menu.

At the bottom of the menu there are two items which are followed by the '^' symbol and a letter. This is fairly standard computerese shorthand for 'hold down the Ctrl key and tap the letter'. Or in the shorthand we have been using in this book, 'Ctrl+(the letter)'. Notation such as this tells you that there is a 'keyboard shortcut' for this particular option. In other words, you don't have to open up the menu at all. So, if you want to blend two objects, you would select them both with the Pick tool and then tap Ctrl+B. (We shall try it out shortly.) You wouldn't see the menu at all. If you think back, you have already used some control codes, for example Ctrl+D to duplicate an object. No menu appeared then, but 'Duplicate' is an option on the edit menu.

Selecting an option from a menu

CD! has many control code shortcuts as well as a range of function key shortcuts. As you get used to working with CD! they will help you speed-up your operations and we are sure that you will use menus less and less.

1 Tap the **Esc** key to cancel the menu (tap it twice if you had selected the sub-menu as well).

We can go on now to look at other methods of selecting items from a menu.

2 Method 1: **CLICK** on the name of the menu, then move the pointer down the menu to the option you want and **CLICK** again when it is highlighted.

Method 2: **CLICK AND HOLD** on the menu name, **DRAG** the highlighting bar down to the option you want and then **RELEASE** the click.

Method 3: Hold down the **Alt** key, tap the underlined letter in the menu name. (You can now release the **Alt** key if you like) and then tap the underlined letter in the name of the option you want.

Method 4: (As we mentioned above) use a control code.

So that's how you select activities from a menu, let's now look properly at the Effects menu.

The Effects menu (Alt-C): Envelopes

The first question that springs to mind is, 'What's an envelope (apart from something you stick a stamp on)?' In CD! terms an envelope is the boundary which follows the shape of a rectangle that encloses an object. When you edit an envelope, CD! enables you to do various things to the shape of the envelope and, therefore, the object:

SQUEEZE   SQUASH   BEND   INCLINE   HIPHOP

These effects are over and above the others we have seen so far. In these examples we have edited the envelope surrounding text, but you can apply the same types of edit to any shape (even a straight line).

As soon as you select one of the editing options, CD! puts a red dotted outline around the bounding rectangle of the object. This outline has eight control points around its perimeter – one on each corner and one in the middle of each side. These behave like a hybrid of the sizing handles generated by the Pick tool and the control nodes on a curve. You edit the shape by grabbing a control handle and moving it in any direction you want. CD! changes the shape of the object to make it fit within the changed bounding box (which may no longer be a rectangle). The precise result you get depends on which form of editing

you have chosen. The sub-menu gives you access to four different kinds of edit. Reading from the top they are: **Straight Line** change, **Single Curved Line** change, **Double Curved Line** change and, what's known as an '**Unconstrained**' change. This does not mean that the shape goes berserk! It means that you have complete control over the shape of the change.

The Effects menu (Alt-C): Envelopes

This result was achieved with a Straight Line edit. We created it by manipulating only the side control points. The same goes for the next two types of edit.

This is a Single Curved Line edit and the next one is a Double Curved Line edit. The last one was produced with an Unconstrained edit.

With the first three types of edit you can use the Ctrl and the SHIFT keys to reshape opposite sides of an image by the same amount. Ctrl causes opposite nodes to move in the same direction, SHIFT causes opposite nodes to move in opposite directions and SHIFT+Ctrl causes all four corners (or sides) to move in opposite directions. Give them a try.

The Effects menu (Alt-C): Envelopes

We got the freeform shape at the bottom of the previous page by moving control handles, like the handles on curve nodes by differing amounts. In the first illustration below, you can see we have already moved the bottom left hand control handle to get the slightly bulbous shape and we are just in the process of positioning the control handles in the bottom side control point.

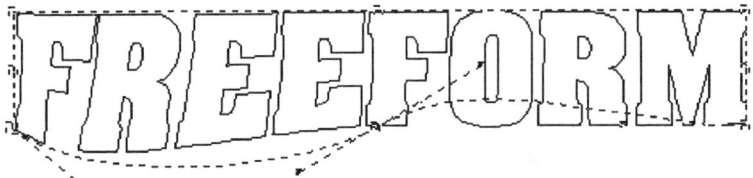

Now, having shaped the top edge, the thing is beginning to take shape and take on a life of its own.

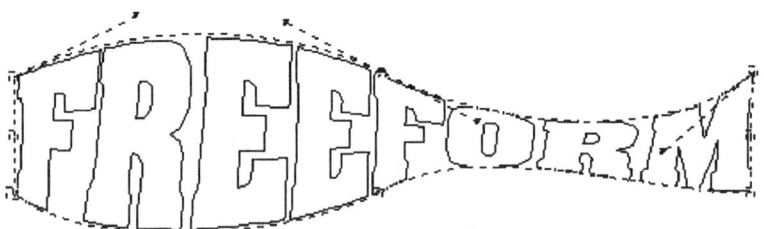

In the last picture you can see what happened when we selected the text with the Pick tool, tapped Ctrl+T to edit the text, changed the wording and then scaled the picture (ho ho! Fish..? Scales..? Oh, never mind).

The Effects menu (Alt-C):
Envelopes

To get this effect – still in unconstrained edit – we selected a number of control points – using marquee select, but we could have used the SHIFT+CLICK method. In all we selected five nodes at the right hand end of the word which enabled us to move the whole section down in one go to get this cascade effect. Well, we like it anyway..!

There is no doubt that using the unconstrained edit mode gives you (and the shapes) a lot of flexibility and we suspect you will want to use it a lot. It is ideal for fitting text into an object which has a complex shape. And it is ideal for creating the complex shape in the first place.

One thing to bear in mind when you are editing the envelopes of several objects is that when you select a particular editing mode, it applies to all the envelopes you are editing. So watch out if you want to have a mix of curved and straight line shapes. Make sure you select the right envelope editing mode when you move between objects. It is easy to forget this point, but if you fall foul of it and find that the flower you are drawing has suddenly acquired straight petals, remember that you can **Undo** the last change you made by tapping **Alt+BACKSPACE**. (This too is fairly standard in Windows applications.)

The Effects menu (Alt-C): Envelopes

If you look down the Effects menu, you will see there are three other options to do with envelopes: **Clear Envelope** (Alt-C-C), which removes the envelope from the object and returns it to its original shape, **Copy Envelope From...** (Alt-C-F) and **Add New Envelope** (Alt-C-N). We shall examine the last of these next.

Sometimes, when you have created a complex object, you may want to change its shape subtly while keeping the same basic shape intact. The way to do this is to add another envelope to the one you have already edited to get your shape. Then you edit the added envelope to get the effect you want. In this way you can combine different editing modes to arrive at the final result.

In this example, Dinosaur Rock, we applied second envelopes to the head shape and to the mouth shapes to get the slight changes you can see in the second version. Finally we exported the whole image to Windows Paintbrush (via the Clipboard) and added shading to the rock. Then we imported the doctored image into Ventura Publisher and produced this page. (Incidentally, we shall be looking at how to use the Windows Clipboard later.) For now we shall continue looking at the options on the Effects menu.

The Effects menu (Alt-C):
Envelopes

The last option to do with envelopes is **Copy Envelope From...** (Alt-C-F). You use this when you want one object to fit the same envelope as another. In the example below we can see this in action as the first stage of fitting some text to a shape which started as a circle.

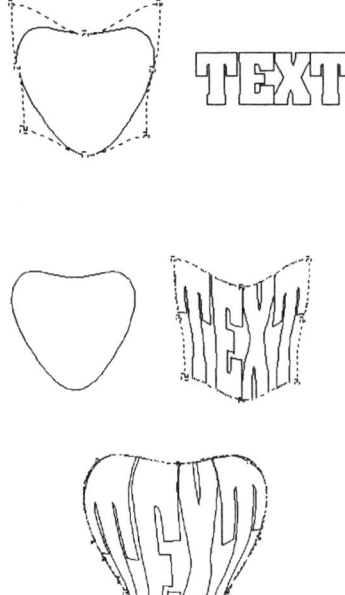

Here we have edited the envelope of the circle to get a strawberry shape. Having done that we selected the text with the Pick tool.

Now we have copied the envelope from the strawberry shape and CD! has automatically redrawn the text. We can go on from here to re-size and reshape the text.

Eventually ending up by editing the text envelope with the unconstrained mode for greater accuracy.

The next block of activities are also to do with one type of effect; Perspective.

The Effects menu (Alt-C): Perspective

1   Clear your page and then create some string text to experiment with. Key-in the word **BLOCK**, in the **Aardvark** typeface, in **72pt**.

2   Open up the **Effects** menu and CLICK on **Edit Perspective**.

You will see a red bounding box appear around your word on screen. The bounding box has a control point at each corner.

3   Grab the bottom left control point, then hold down the **Ctrl** key and drag the control point slowly downwards (CD! will constrain you to a vertical movement) and watch the right hand side of the screen.

You will see an X shape appear and move inwards as you move the control point down.

4   Get the **X** on the work page and then RELEASE the click.

CD! immediately redraws the text with perspective added. The X marks the 'Vanishing Point' for the perspective which CD! has applied to your text.

You can use this vanishing point to alter the perspective as well.

The Effects menu (Alt-C): Perspective

5   Grab the vanishing point, and gently move it to the right and to the left. Watch what happens to the bounding box. Then try moving the vanishing point upwards and downwards.

The changes you have seen are single point perspective, where the object seems to recede away in one plane only. But, with CD! you can also have two point perspective, where the object seems to recede in two planes.

6   Grab the bottom left control point again and this time hold down **Ctrl** and **SHIFT**. Move the control point slowly down and left. Watch the top of the screen.

You will see a second vanishing point appear on the screen. When you release the click the text will redraw and it will seem to be receding from right to left and from front to back.

7   Tap the **SPACEBAR**, then tap **Alt-C-L** to clear the perspective (another option on the Effects menu). Then try editing the perspective a few times – clearing each time it gets too complicated to fathom out. Editing perspective is very easy to do, but it took us a while to get the feel of it.

The two remaining perspective options, **Copy Perspective from...** and **Add New Perspective** fulfil the same functions for perspective as the similarly named options higher up the menu performed for Envelopes, so we shall leave things there and move on to the next option.

The Effects menu (Alt-C): Blend

This is one of those effects you really must see for yourself! So work through the following steps and we will discuss them afterwards.

1 Clear the work page, then draw a good sized 'landscape' rectangle. Put an ellipse in the rectangle, in the top right hand quadrant, with its long axis vertical. Fill the ellipse with white and the rectangle with red.

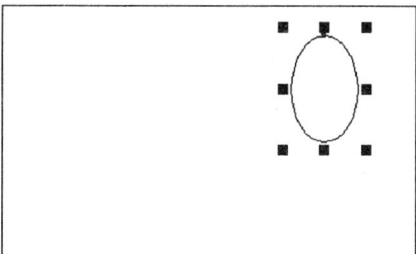

2 With the Pick tool, **SHIFT CLICK** to select both objects. Then either tap **Ctrl+B** or tap **Alt-C-B**.

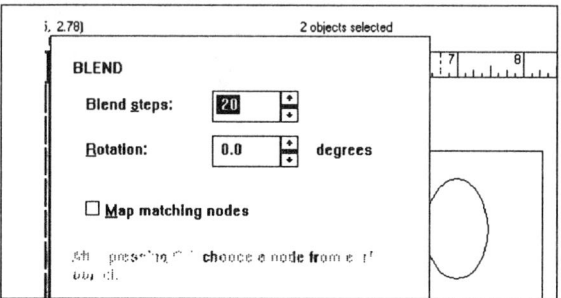

3 Just accept CD!'s default settings by clicking on **OK**.

That triggers the first visual experience. Your screen should look something like this.

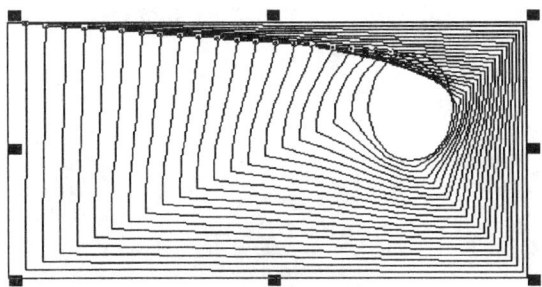

But now get a full page preview and you will see the real visual for yourself. Black and white reproduction does not do it justice, but, just for the record, here it is anyway.

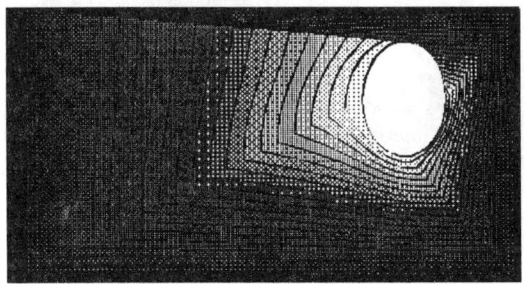

On your screen you will probably have 22 slightly different outlines creating a gradual blend from red to white and from a large rectangle to a small ellipse. But now try this:

4   Get back to the work page and **marquee select** all the objects. Then **cancel their outlines** lines via the pen nib icon.

The Effects menu (Alt-C):
Blend

5 Now get another full page preview.

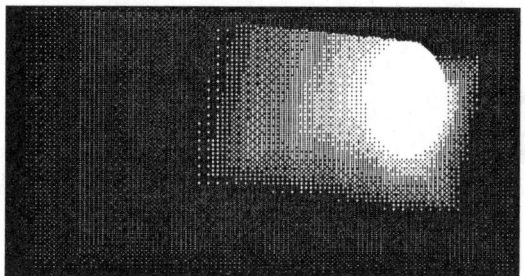

Try giving the shapes different outline colours to see the effects you can get. Then cancel their outlines again and give the objects a radial fill from red to white. It takes a long time to draw, but the effect is quite impressive.

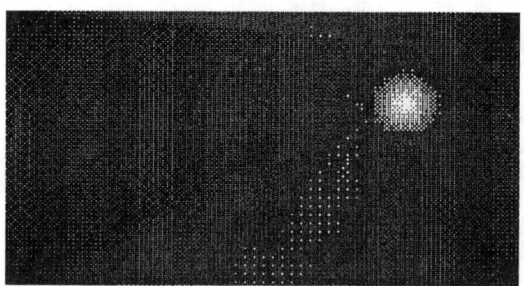

The dialog box for creating blends enables you to change the number of steps between blends and to add rotation to the blend process. The first of these is pretty well self explanatory, but to us the word 'rotation' conjures up a picture of an object tumbling, or rotating about a centre point. This is not what happens, as you can see at the top of the next page. The objects do not rotate, instead the path of the transformations acquires a curve.

The Effects menu (Alt-C): Blend

To get this type of effect, we first of all created the three string text objects. Then we coloured them red, white and red. We marquee selected 'TIME' and 'AND' then clicked again on one of their outlines to activate rotate and skew mode. This enabled us to drag the centre of rotation for the two objects up and to the right.

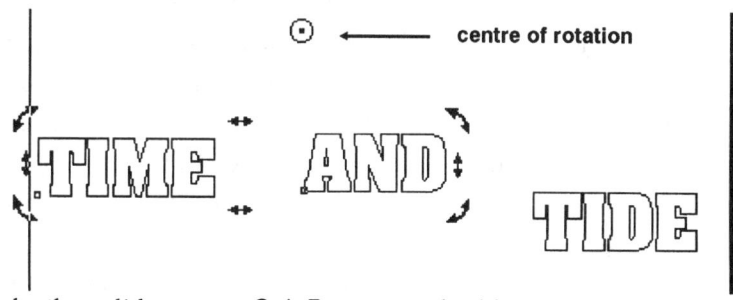

Only then did we tap Ctrl+B to start the blend process. When the dialog box appeared, we amended the Rotation value to 45 degrees and tapped RETURN. Then we repeated the process for AND and TIDE, except we moved the centre of rotation down and slightly left. We ended up with a confusing mish-mash which we tidied up by moving the three original objects slightly.

The Effects menu (Alt-C): Blend

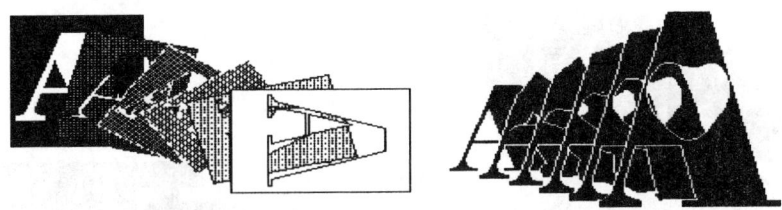

In these two examples of blend effects we have reduced the number of blend steps to four. But we have also done something else which we shall be discussing shortly in the sections on the Arrange menu; we have created 'cutouts' on the figures. Notice you can see through the objects. This effect is very easy to generate, but it does involve a particular procedure which we do not want to cover now.

There is one further item on the blend dialog box you need to know about: 'Map matching nodes'. If you created one object by pulling right and the second by pulling left, then you might get some funny results when you blend, so CD! allows you to tell it which nodes to map to. The illustration below shows two blend processes. In both cases we started by creating two rectangles, one pulled to the right and the other pulled to the left. In the first example on the left, we did not map matching nodes, but in the second we told CD! to match to the start node for each rectangle. So, this is something else worth playing with to see the different results you can get.

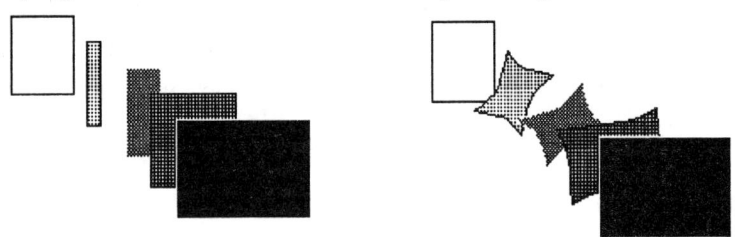

The Effects menu (Alt-C): Extrude

1 Clear your work page, then, on the left hand side of the page, draw a square with circle sitting on it.

2 With the Pick tool, select one of the objects, then either tap **Alt-C-X** or **Ctrl+E** to activate the Extrude option. As usual you will get a dialog box.

By this stage of the game you will know how to use the dialog box, so we shall make very few points about it, other than saying don't worry about 'Absolute Coordinates' and 'Scaling Factor' for the moment. Let us look at the basic settings first.

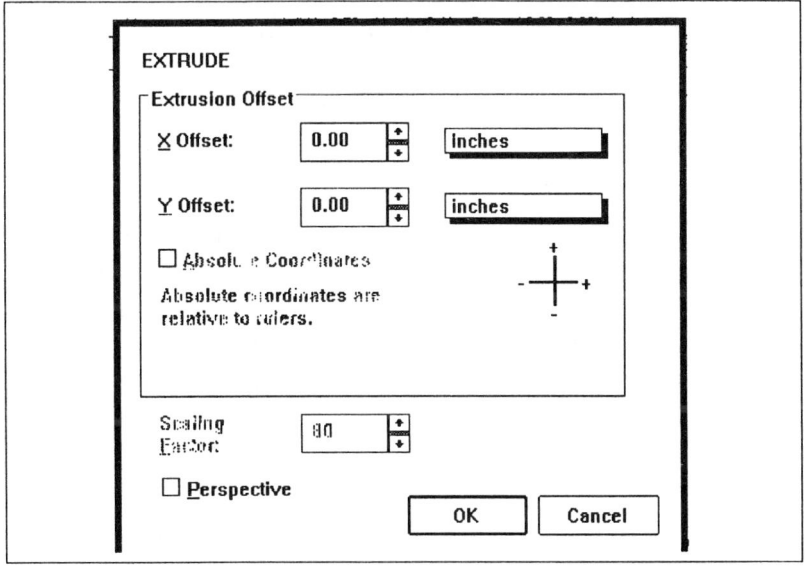

Fig. 5-2 **Specifying the Extrude settings.**

The Effects menu (Alt-C): Extrude

3 Set the **X Offset** (the X offset is "a cross" the page (geddit?) – though why they can't say horizontal offset, defeats us) to **2 inches** (or 50.8mm... or 12 picas, point... or 144pt, depending on which measurement system you prefer).

4 Set the **Y Offset** (offset **vertically**) to **1 inch** and CLICK on OK.

5 Now select the other object and give it the same settings.

When you make these settings, a positive value moves the horizontal offset to the right (negative to the left) and a positive value moves the vertical offset upwards (negative downwards).

What we want you to do next is to copy the transformed objects. You can do this in several ways – e.g. you can marquee select the whole image, then tap Ctrl+D to duplicate it, or the easier way (from version 2.01 of CD!) is to simply tap the number pad + key to put a second copy of the image behind the first, then move one of the images to the right hand side of the page. You can get the same effect by grabbing the image then clicking the right mouse button as you move the image to its new position (i.e. click the right mouse button without releasing the grab).

When you have your second copy on the page:

1 De-select the objects by clicking on a blank part of the page.

2   Working on your copy, select the extruded portion of the square component of the image. In the status area, CD! tells you you have selected a group of 2 objects. Tap the **Delete** key to get rid of the two objects which make up the extrusion, leaving the square intact.

3   Now do the same for the extruded part of the circle – Notice that this is also a group of 2 objects.

4   Next select one of the objects and activate the Extrude option again.

You will notice that the offset settings still reflect the values you gave them just now.

5   Click on the little square labelled **Perspective**. Set the **Scaling Factor** to **50**, then CLICK on OK.

The Scaling Factor determines the position of the vanishing point. The closer the factor number is to zero the further the extrusion seems to recede. For numbers between 0 and 99 the vanishing point is behind the object (so it seems to recede into the distance). The value 100 has no effect, but numbers between 101 and 400 place the vanishing point in front of the object so it seems to advance towards the viewer. With the vanishing point in front of the object the higher the number, the more it seems to advance.

The Effects menu (Alt-C): Extrude

6   Repeat the exercise for your second object.

What a mess! CD! has added the same perspective for both objects, that is, it has created two different vanishing points when normally we expect one. You can get around this by using the <u>A</u>bsolute Coordinates option on the dialog box to position the vanishing point. But, be aware, when you do this, the X and Y coordinates no longer take their start point from the position of the objects. Instead, with our current settings, the vanishing point (for both objects) will be placed where the 2 inch mark is on the horizontal ruler (assuming you have set the rulers – see later) and where the 1 inch mark is on the vertical ruler. There is a quicker, but less accurate way of getting the result we want.

1   Delete the two extruded portions again, to leave the original square and circle.

Note

If you delete the wrong thing by mistake, don't panic! Instead, simply tap **Alt+BACKSPACE** to 'Undo' the last action you took. CD! will restore the bit you didn't mean to change. This is a general rule which applies at all times in CD! (and whenever you are working in Windows).

2   Marquee select both objects and then tap **Ctrl+C**.

Ctrl+C combines the two objects into one, so when we apply our perspective extrusion CD! will generate only one vanishing point.

3   Tap **Ctrl+E** then RETURN to add a perspective extrusion to our new image.

You will not see the dialog box, because you have bypassed it with this quick way of implementing commands; Alt-C-X-RETURN would have done the same thing.

4   Now, CLICK on one of the colour tablets on the screen palette (but we'll use a fountain fill). Then get a page preview.

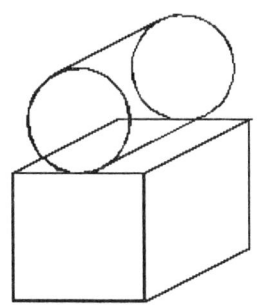

Notice the square has become a square tube you can see through. This is because the original image(s) had no fill ... and areas with no fill are transparent in a combined object

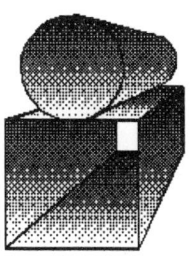

such as this, so you can see where the other end of the square tube intrudes into the top right corner of the original square. The circular tube looks solid because you cannot see the far end through the near end. Check by looking at the work page. This phenomenon is the basis for producing the 'cutouts' we mentioned a short while ago.

The Arrange menu (Alt-A): Overview

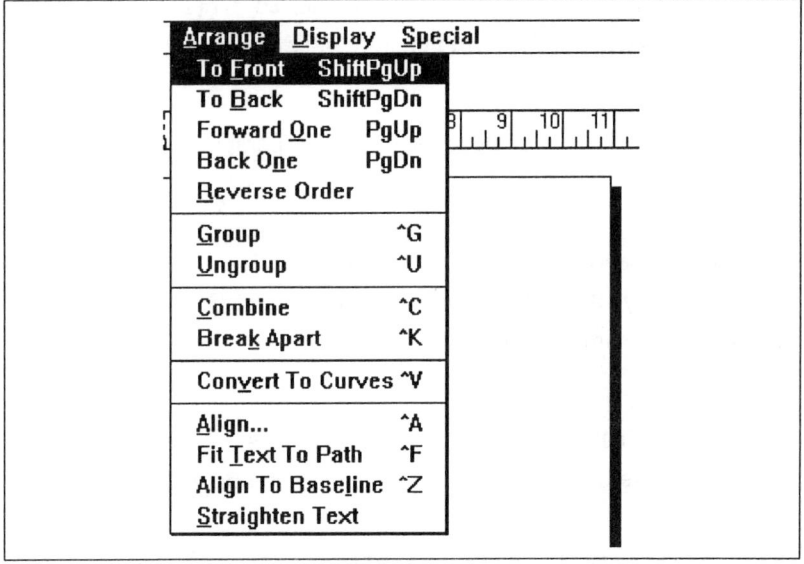

Fig. 5-3 **The arrange menu options.**

As its name suggests this menu enables you to arrange objects in various ways. The first block lets you arrange the sequence of objects on the page. The second block lets you arrange objects in groups, or to ungroup them. The third block lets you combine two or more objects into one – you will recognise the Ctrl+C command, because we used it just now when we were looking at perspective extrusions. You can also break combined objects apart when you want to. The fourth item, 'Convert To Curves', indirectly allows you to arrange the shape of an object, and the fifth and last block enables you to arrange text in various ways. In the next few sections we shall examine each of these blocks of activities in turn.

The Arrange menu (Alt-A): Sequencing images

When you create images that overlap, you sometimes get some odd effects, like the sun rising in front of the pyramid in your desert scene. This is because CD! draws the objects in the sequence you created them. So, if you drew the sun after you drew the pyramid, the sun will be 'stacked' on top of the pyramid. It is not always possible, and often inconvenient, to draw objects in the right sequence. So, the Arrange menu, as well as some keyboard shortcuts, give you control over where images are placed in the stack.

We created this image by creating the letters **E,P** and **A** as separate items of string text, in that order. We then gave each one a different fill and moved them around to get this image.

The next stage was to select the E and move it **to the front** of the stack via the Arrange menu (or with **Alt-A-F**, or SHIFT+ the **Page Up** key).

After this we selected the P and moved it **one forward** via the menu (or with **Alt-A-O**, or the **Page Up** key).

Finally we moved the E **back one** via the menu (or with **Alt-A-N** or **Page Down**). We could have got exactly the same end result if we'd simply started by moving the A **to the back** via the menu (or with **Alt-A-B** or SHIFT+**Page Down**).

The Arrange menu (Alt-A): Group v Combine images

Grouping and combining images are similar activities, but there are some significant differences. Broadly speaking, you group or combine images when you want to process the component parts together. Of course, you can do the same thing by marquee selecting several objects for processing, but you will have to do it every time you want to make a change. When you group the objects they stay grouped together until you ungroup them again.

Even so, it is best to think of grouping objects as being a temporary device, while combining them is a bit more permanent. A group of three objects is still three objects, each retaining their own characteristics. On the other hand, combining three objects creates one new object, with one set of characteristics. You can see one aspect of this in the following patterns. The outline shapes are all the same.

On the left are the original three objects. We grouped these together to get the second image. Notice, the component objects have not changed their appearance. The third image is the three objects combined into a single object. Now it has one fill. For the fourth image we gave the group a fountain fill, simply to demonstrate that you can treat a group as a single object if you want to. But notice that the three original components each have their own fountain fill. You would get quite a different result with the combined object. For a start, it would have one fountain fill and where the letters overlapped you would get transparent 'holes' through the image.

The Arrange menu (Alt-A): Group v Combine images

Another difference occurs when you dis-assemble a group and a combined image. When you Ungroup an image you simply return the objects to their previous status, but when you Break a combined image Apart you actually break it into components and sub components. This next illustration shows you what we mean.

The top row of letters was originally three lots of string text which we combined into a single object. We then used Ctrl+K to Break the image Apart again. Then we selected the objects. But then, instead of three lots of string text, we seemed to have six individual letters, so we SHIFT-CLICKED on their outlines to select all of them. Then we moved the selected letters down a bit and got the result you can see in the second row. The triangles and the ellipses above the filled-in letters used to be the cut-outs in the letters. Breaking the single image apart has also broken the individual letters apart, so we ended up with 12 objects. Had we marquee selected all the objects, this problem would not have been apparent, but it would have been real enough – lurking there to catch us unawares some time later.

The Arrange menu (Alt-A): Combining images

The upshot, as far as we are concerned, is that the act of grouping objects produces results we would have expected, but combining produces different results. It is because it produces different results that combining objects is so interesting and useful. The key point to remember is that when you combine a set of objects, they become one 'curve' object.

If you think back to when we were experimenting with editing curve nodes, you might remember we talked about joining and aligning nodes on separate objects. We made the point then that you first have to make the objects into one (by tapping Ctrl+C to combine them – via this option). Only then can you select the nodes you want to join or align (because you can't select nodes from separate objects). So that is one way in which combining objects can help you, but there are others. For example, when you combine several objects into one, the combined image takes up far less memory space than the separate images, so that improves CD!'s performance.

But perhaps the most spectacular benefit of combining objects is the one we have already mentioned a couple of times, the facility to create cut-outs (or 'masks', depending on how you want to look at the end result).

You will remember the image we created during the Merge exercises – we've repeated it at the top of the next page, to remind you. This image has the two original objects (shapes), plus a group of twenty transitional shapes.

The Arrange menu (Alt-A):
Combining images

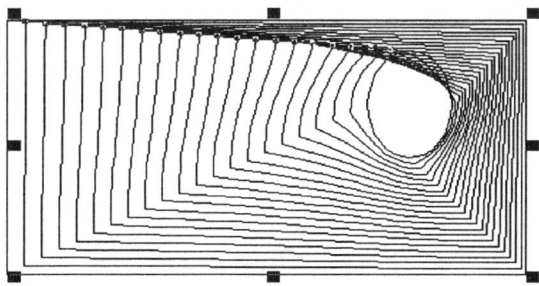

We ungrouped the shapes and then we combined them all into one object. Then we applied a fill to the object...

This, by itself is an interesting result, alternate bands of fill and white, but when you realise that the white bands are transparent...

You begin to see some fascinating possibilities for graphic effects.

We have created a few more images on the next page which exploit this phenomenon.

The Arrange menu (Alt-A)
Combining images

A kettle advertisement, using the transparency phenomenon.

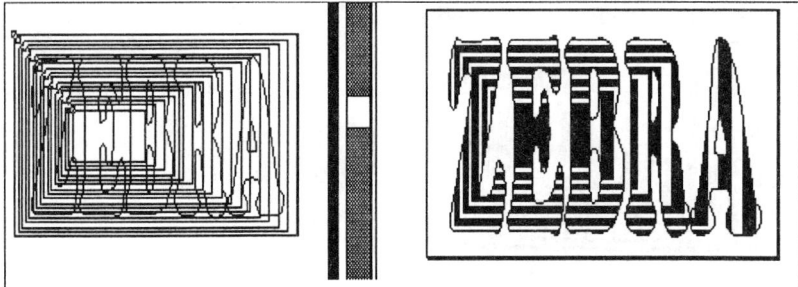

To create the image on the right we first of all blended two rectangles, ungrouped them, combined them and gave them a fill to get the striped effect. Then we combined text and a rectangle, gave the object a white fill and laid it, as a mask, on the striped image.

For this one we gave the mask a white fill and no outline.

The Arrange menu (Alt-A)
Convert to curves

When you create rectangles, ellipses and string text you can modify or transform these objects in a variety of ways. But there is a limit to the things you can do with such objects. Sometimes you will want to massage the shapes a bit more, to get a very precise image, not normally possible with the standard effects for the object.

The way to do this is to convert the objects to curves, which then opens up the extra controls you can exploit by using the Shaping tool. Bear in mind, though, that once you have converted your objects into curves you cannot convert them back again (except by using Alt+BACKSPACE or Alt-E-U immediately after you have made the change). Let us see how this option extends our shaping powers.

1 Draw a **rectangle** and an **ellipse**, then add the word **ShipShape**, in string text. Make the text **72pt**, in the **Arabia** typeface.

2 With the **Shaping tool**, CLICK on each of the three objects in turn, simply to remind yourself of the normal shaping options open to you.

3 With the **Pick tool**, select one of the objects. Then, either, open up the **Arrange** menu and select the **Convert To Curves** option... or, tap Alt-A-V... or, tap Ctrl+V. Then do the same for the other two objects. (You have to convert one object at a time.)

The Arrange menu (Alt-A): Convert to curves

4 With the **Shaping tool** again, select each of the objects in turn and look at the difference.

Notice that the ellipse now has four nodes rather than one. The rectangle still has four nodes, but when you experiment you will find they behave in a quite different way from the normal nodes. As for the word ShipShape, well this seems to have acquired a Penicillin like coating of nodes.

These new nodes are curve nodes and, as such, are capable of being manipulated in all the ways we examined earlier when we looked at the Shaping tool.

Here, for example, are the shapes we drew during the exercise and then subsequently altered a bit. The rectangle is at the left, then the ellipse. The string text is still recognisable. See if you can get similar results.

The Arrange menu (Alt-A): Align objects

The menu offers various ways of aligning things with each other and we shall look at each option, starting with the cryptic sounding **Align...** option. To use this option, you begin by selecting the object (or objects) you want to align (with the Pick tool). Then you either open up the menu and select the option, or tap Alt-A-A, or tap Ctrl+A. You will get the following dialog box.

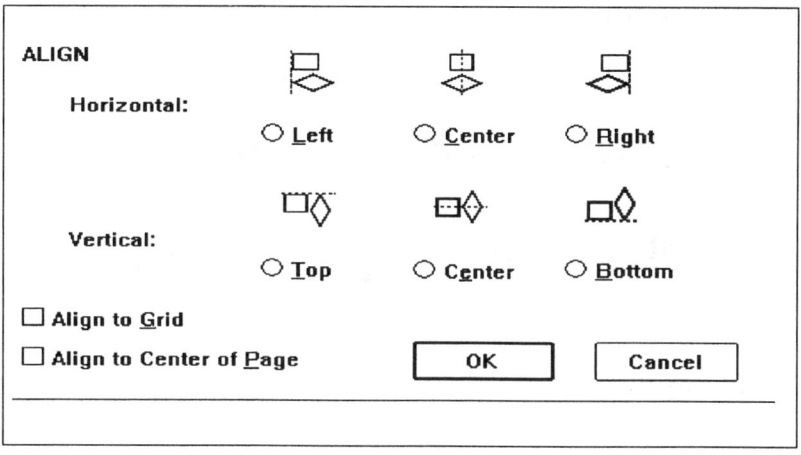

Fig. 5-4 **The Align dialog box.**

We found this a bit confusing at first, because there is too much information on the screen. About half of the information in the main body of the box is there to tell you how to use the settings, which you select via the radio buttons. There are two rows of radio buttons, one to control the horizontal alignment of objects and the other to control their vertical alignment. The little 'box and diamond' icons are meant to illustrate the effect of each radio button.

The Arrange menu (Alt-A): Align objects

Unfortunately, notwithstanding the confusing icons, the dialog box still lacks one key piece of information; you can select two alignment settings (one horizontal and one vertical) at the same time, if you want.

For example, as the right hand side of following diagram shows, you could choose to align two objects to their vertical centre point **and** their horizontal centre point (as well as other combinations).

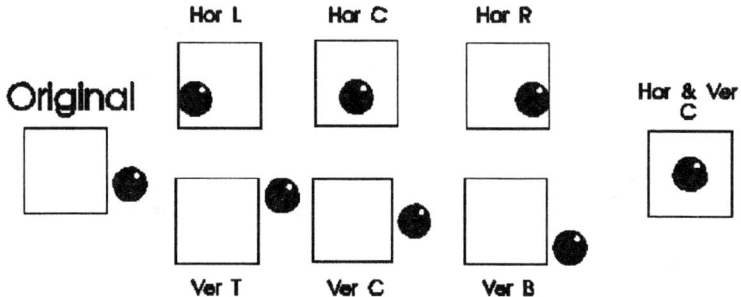

In this illustration we started off at the left with two objects, a square and a billiard ball. In the top row of three configurations, we aligned the objects to different horizontal settings and in the bottom row we changed their vertical alignments. On the right, we set both horizontal and vertical alignments.

You will notice two other settings on the dialog box: Align to Grid and Align to Center of Page. The 'Grid' referred to is one which you can ask CD! to provide, to help you position objects – more of that when we examine the Display menu. The 'Center of Page' is, we would guess, self explanatory, in that the centre of the object is placed at the centre of the page.

The Arrange menu (Alt-A):
Fit Text to a path

Once again, the best way to describe this option is to show you how it works. This next illustration shows two items of string text and two objects. The circle we created by pulling down and right, the curve was also pulled to the right. 'So, what!?' you might say. Well it does make a difference as we shall demonstrate shortly.

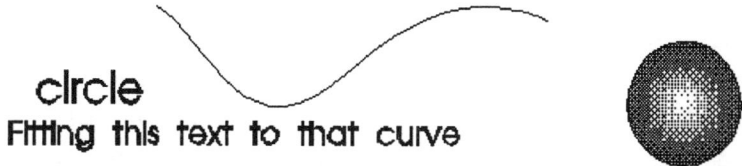

The second illustration shows what happens when we select an object and an item of text and then tap Ctrl+F, or tap Alt-A-T, or open up the menu and select the Fit Text To Path option. We did this for the word 'circle' and the circle object and for the other two items.

For the next two illustrations overleaf we created string text as before and then created two ellipses (one pulled up and left and the other, down and left). We also created the curve by pulling left. Then we fitted the text to the various paths.

Have a look at the results. (N.B. The 'EGG' ellipse is the one we pulled down and left.)

The Arrange menu (Alt-A)
Fitting text to a path

So, you can get different results by creating the objects in different ways. And once you have aligned the text you still have many controls open to you to adjust and fine tune your image. (See page 242 in your CD! User's Manual for the detailed rules, e.g. the effects of justification.) In our examples we have not deleted the objects which provided the path for the alignment operation. This is perhaps the most obvious adjustment you can make to get results like this.

But what if you change your mind and decide that your text doesn't really create the effect you want? The bottom item on the Arrange menu, Straighten Text, comes galloping to the rescue. You simply select the text, then either open up the menu and make your selection, or tap-in Alt-A-S. After a moments thought, CD! straightens everything up again.

The last remaining item on the Arrange menu, Align To Baseline, enables you to tidy up your text after you have moved or re-sized individual letters. As its name suggests, this option aligns the bottoms of the letters with the imaginary line on which they stand.

The Transform menu (Alt-T):
Introduction

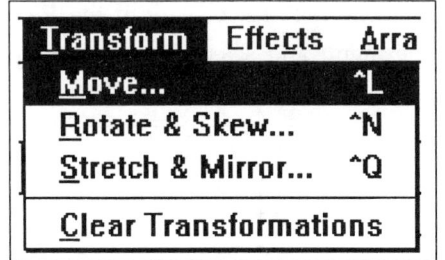

Fig. 5-5 **Transform options.**

Apart from one option on this menu, the last one, you have already done all the activities. You did them 'dynamically', or 'interactively', or 'manually' – in other words, by eye. But this menu lets you do things by numbers, which, we suppose, ought to be more accurate. Notice that the first three options on the menu all end with three dots. This tells you they all lead on to dialog boxes. The last item on the menu, Clear transformations, is the only one not to have a control code shortcut or any dots.

Now, this strikes us as a bit daft, because we use control codes whenever we can to speed things up. And, because we're always trying to work as quickly as possible, we quite often have to go back to the drawing board after we have tried out some new effect.

So for us, a control code which would cancel out our latest experiments – our latest set of transformations – on an object, would have been very useful indeed. Still, there's no point dreaming, there just isn't a control code and that's that! So, let us look at the three other options.

The Transform menu (Alt-T): Move...

1 Draw an object, or create some text, select it with the **Pick tool** and then open up the menu and select **Move...** (or tap Ctrl+L, or Alt-T-M).

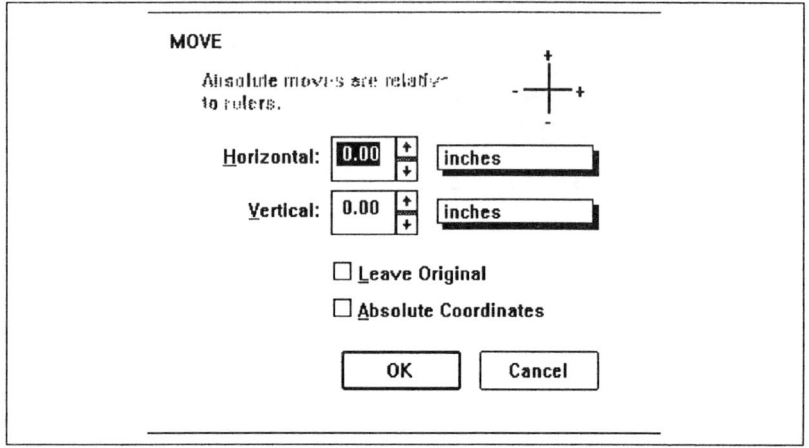

Fig. 5-6 **The Move dialog box.**

You can move an object in two ways with this dialog box. You can either move it by a certain amount vertically and/or horizontally from its present position, or you can move it to a precise position by setting coordinates determined by ruler measurements (i.e. CD!'s on-screen rulers – the settings of which can change). If you want to position the object by its ruler coordinates you have to begin by clicking on the little box labelled Absolute Coordinates (or by tapping the letter A). You will then be asked to specify which part of the object should be aligned to the coordinates. The numbers you enter in the horizontal and vertical settings boxes will then be interpreted by CD! as ruler coordinates.

The Transform menu (Alt-T): Move...

We shall not do that, though. Instead, we shall move the object from its present position by a certain amount. We shall move it horizontally to the right by 1 inch and we shall move it down by 2 inches.

2 Set the **Horizontal:** measurement to **1.00 inches** and the **Vertical:** measurement to **-2.00 inches**, CLICK on **Leave Original** and then CLICK on OK.

You will now have two copies of your object, one at the original location and another below and to the right of the original. The copy will be selected for processing.

You achieved the same effect 'dynamically' by selecting the object with the Pick tool. Then you clicked and held on the outline of the object and started to drag it to its new position. Before you fixed the object in its new position you clicked the right hand mouse button, or tapped the grey + sign in the number pad, to leave the original behind.

We will leave you to decide which method you prefer.

The Transform menu (Alt-T): Rotate & Skew...

1 Draw an object, or create some text, select it with the **Pick tool** and then open up the menu and select **Rotate & Skew** (or tap Ctrl+N, or Alt-T-R).

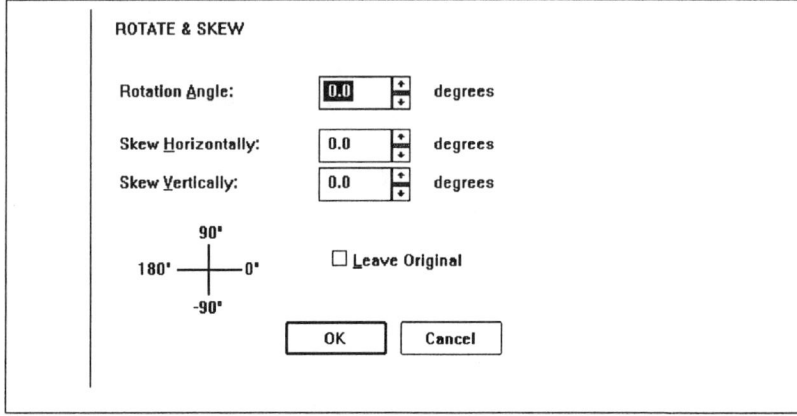

Fig. 5-7 **The Rotate & Skew dialog box.**

We doubt if there is much that needs explaining about this dialog box. It is best if you experiment with it by yourself. There are one or two points to note, though.

You will notice that if you adjust the Rotation Angle, then you will not be able to adjust the skew at the same time. Likewise, if you change either of the Skew angle settings you will not be able to rotate the image. Also, any rotation you set, will be about the natural centre point of the object, unless you move the centre point manually before selecting this activity. The compass points in the bottom left of the dialog box tells you how CD! will interpret your angle settings.

The Transform menu (Alt-T): Stretch & Mirror...

1 Draw an object, or create some text, select it with the **Pick tool** and then open up the menu and select **Stretch & Mirror** (or tap Ctrl+Q, or Alt-T-S).

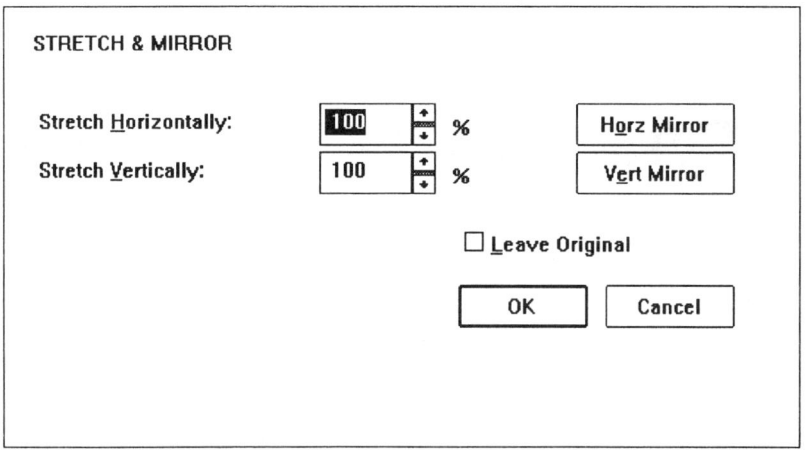

STRETCH & MIRROR

Stretch **H**orizontally: [100] ⬍ %   [**H**orz Mirror]

Stretch **V**ertically: [100] ⬍ %   [**V**ert Mirror]

☐ **L**eave Original

[OK]   [Cancel]

Fig. 5-8 **The Stretch & Mirror dialog box.**

This dialog box needs even less explanation than the last one, so we shall simply leave you to try it out for yourself... Except, there is perhaps one thing which might throw you. The percentage stretch settings do not change things **by** a certain amount. They change things **to** a percentage of the object's present size. So if you select 50% horizontal stretch you will not increase the size by half, you will reduce it **to** half.

The Edit menu (Alt-E): Overview

1   Begin by drawing a rectangle in the lower right quadrant of the work page. Then add some string text, in **72pt** just above it.

2   Select the rectangle with the **Pick tool**, skew the rectangle by about 15 degrees to the left (remember the Ctrl, 'constrain', key), and then open up the **Edit** menu.

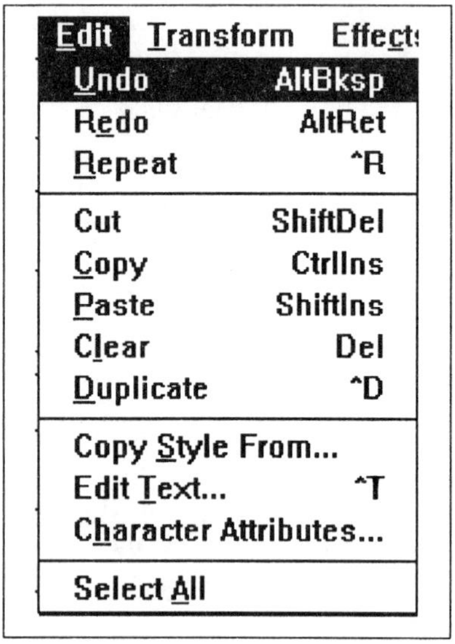

Edit	**Transform**	**Effect**
Undo		**AltBksp**
R**e**do		**AltRet**
R**e**peat		**^R**
Cut		**ShiftDel**
Copy		**CtrlIns**
Paste		**ShiftIns**
Cl**e**ar		**Del**
Duplicate		**^D**
Copy **S**tyle From...		
Edit **T**ext...		**^T**
C**h**aracter Attributes...		
Select **A**ll		

Fig. 5-9   **The Edit options.**

The first two items on the menu are counterparts to each other. The first one cancels, or undoes the last action you took. So, if you select it now, you will see the rectangle return to its original shape.

The menu will disappear from the screen at the same time, but you can still use the one on the left here to refresh your memory. If you now hold down the Alt key and tap the RETURN key, you will see your rectangle skew again.

3   When you are fed up with animating, leave the rectangle skewed. Select your text and then tap **Ctrl+R** and watch what happens.

The Edit menu (Alt-E): Cut, Copy & Paste

So, the third item on the menu, shortcut code Ctrl+R, repeats the last transformation you made to an object. And it repeats it for any object. Moving on now to the second block of activities on the menu:

1 With the rectangle still selected and without the menu on screen, hold down a **SHIFT** key, tap the **Delete** key and watch the screen.

CD! seems to think for a moment and then you see a message telling you that the destination for the thing you have 'Cut' (with SHIFT+Delete) is the Windows Clipboard. The rectangle also disappears from the work page. You can paste the object back onto the work page, or into another file, providing you do not put anything else on the clipboard in the meantime. And, don't forget, you can 'Undo' the most recent action as well.

2 Hold down a **SHIFT** key and tap the **Insert** key, to paste the rectangle back on the page.

Notice it reappears in exactly the same position. This may not be very surprising when you are simply pasting the object back into the same file, but it is also true when you paste it into another file, which is something to remember if you are working on different sized drawings.

3 Now tap the paste key combination again.

The Edit menu (Alt-E):
Cut, Copy & Paste

Nothing seems to have happened, but ...

4 Grab the outline of the rectangle and move it up and to the left.

When you release the mouse button, you will see that the first skewed rectangle you pasted-in is still in position. So this is another way of duplicating an object.

5 Tap the **Delete** key on its own to get rid of one of the rectangles.

(The Undo command would bring it back, provided you did nothing else before invoking the command, but tapping Delete on its own does not put a copy on the clipboard. If you used the paste keys again now you would get another copy of the skewed rectangle, which is not what we want, so we won't do it.)

6 Select the string text you keyed in. Now, hold down the **Ctrl** key and tap **Insert**.

After a short pause you will get that 'destination' message again, but this time the object (your string text) stays where it is. The Ctrl+Insert key combination also puts a copy of the object(s) on the Windows Clipboard, but it merely copies whatever you had selected. It does not cut the object(s) from the file as the SHIFT+Delete combination does.

The Edit menu (Alt-E): Clear and Duplicate

7 To prove this, move the text to one side and then tap SHIFT+**Insert** to paste the contents of the clipboard into the file. The text will reappear in the place you copied it from.

Whether you use the Copy command or the Cut command (notice there is no Alt code sequence of keys for Cut – none of the letters is underlined!), the Paste function allows you to create many duplicate copies of an object. As long as you do not put anything else on the clipboard, you can paste an object as often as you like and so make as many copies as you like. But you will remember from earlier in the book that there are two much easier ways of getting the same end result:

- Grab an object, then as you move it, either tap the grey + key in the number pad, or click the right hand mouse button

- Tap Ctrl+D to invoke the Duplicate option from this menu.

1 Select your rectangle and tap **Ctrl+D** to duplicate it.

2 Now tap **Ctrl+R** a few times. We can build on this effect, by holding down the SHIFT key and stretching the selected rectangle from one corner by a small amount. Tap the **grey + key**, before you release the mouse button. Now tap **Ctrl+R** a few more times.

Don't get confused between Ctrl+D and Ctrl+R; the first duplicates the selected **object,** while the other duplicates (repeats) the last **command**.

The Edit menu (Alt-E):
Copy Style From...

Before we look at the third block on the menu, we want you to use the very last option – Select All – to help us clear the way.

1 Either, tap **Alt-E-A,** or, open up the menu and select the last item. CD! will select every object on the page for processing. Then tap the **Delete** key to get rid of them all in one go.

2 If you tap the **Paste** combination of keys (SHIFT+Insert), you should get your text back, because that was the last thing you put on the clipboard when you worked through the previous pages. Now create another rectangle.

We'll make some changes to the text then apply them to the rectangle.

3 With the **Pick tool**, select the text. Open up the outlines fly-out menu and select the line thickness which is sixth from the right. Now select the pure red colour for the fill (left mouse button) and a pure blue for the line colour (right button). Get a full page preview to check that your rectangle looks quite different from the text. If, by chance, it has the same colourings and line thicknesses, change those for the text.

4 Select the rectangle (because you want to copy its new style from something else), then tap **Alt-E-S** to select the option.

The Edit menu (Alt-E): Copy Style From...

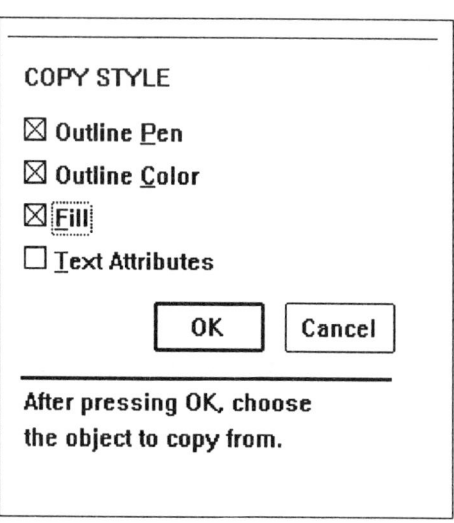

COPY STYLE

☒ Outline Pen
☒ Outline Color
☒ Fill
☐ Text Attributes

| OK | Cancel |

After pressing OK, choose
the object to copy from.

You will get this dialog box. Notice we have clicked on the top three boxes to tell CD! which elements of the style we want to copy from our text.

Fig. 5-10 **The Copy Style From... Dialog box.**

5 CLICK on the same three buttons, then CLICK on OK. CD! will display a black arrow on which is written the message, 'From?'. Move the point of the arrow onto the outline of the text and CLICK.

If you miss the outline, CD! will offer you the chance to try again.

6 Get another full page preview to see the result.

The Edit menu (Alt-E):
Edit Text

This option enables you to change the text itself and to change the attributes (settings) for the whole text, as opposed to the next option we shall examine which allows you to change the attributes for individual letters.

1 Select the text, then either tap **Alt-E-T**, or **Ctrl+T** or open up the menu and select the option.

After a short pause, CD! displays the text entry screen we saw when we looked at creating text.

2 Select the **Bodnoff** typeface and set the size to **108pt**. Then **CLICK** on **OK**.

You will see the changes implemented for all the text. But the changes have been made only to the actual components of the text – the raw material for the object. If you get a full page preview, you will see that the <u>style</u> of the text object remains the same, even though its contents have changed.

The Edit menu (Alt-E)
Character Attributes...

The key word to notice in this option is 'Character'. In other words, this option allows you to make a range of changes to individual characters within the text. But first you have to select the character, or characters you want to tweak.

1 Select the **Shaping tool**. Then CLICK on the outline of the text.

CD! will display the nodes, and the character space and line space arrows.

2 SHIFT CLICK on the nodes for the first and the last characters in your text (at the bottom left of the characters). Tap **Alt-E-H**, or open up the menu and select the option.

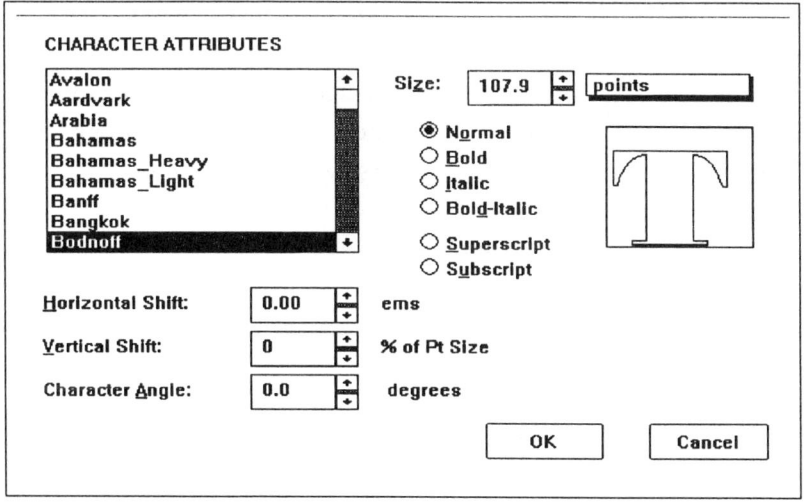

Fig. 5-11 **Changing the attributes of individual characters.**

The Edit menu (Alt-E)
Character Attributes...

N.B. You can also select the option by double clicking on a node.

The dialog for this option is reminiscent of the text entry box we saw just now, but there are some key differences as you will see from the illustration on the previous page. Any settings you specify in this box will apply only to the two characters you have selected.

3 Change the typeface to **Aardvark**, set the size to **144pt** and set the vertical shift to **-20%** (i.e. move them down by 20%).

4 CLICK on OK and look at the end result.

5 Finally, get a full page preview to see the full effect.

So, remember, if you want to make changes which will apply to all of a text object, use the Pick tool and then take the Edit Text option. If you want to make changes to letters within a text object, use the Shaping tool.

You can use the last two options we have examined on both string and paragraph text.

The Display menu (Alt-D)

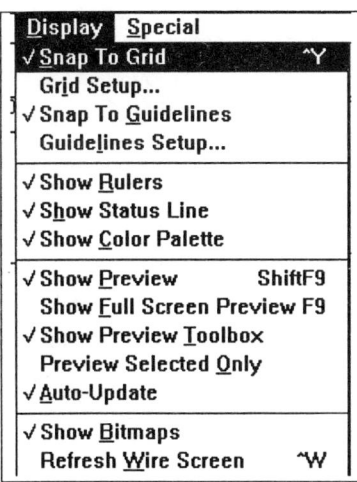

Display	Special	
√ Snap To Grid		^Y
Grid Setup...		
√ Snap To Guidelines		
Guidelines Setup...		
√ Show Rulers		
√ Show Status Line		
√ Show Color Palette		
√ Show Preview		ShiftF9
Show Full Screen Preview		F9
√ Show Preview Toolbox		
Preview Selected Only		
√ Auto-Update		
√ Show Bitmaps		
Refresh Wire Screen		^W

This menu is different from the others we have seen so far because it controls CD! itself rather than what is done to an object or an image. The majority of options are straightforward on/off settings which do not call for a great deal of explanation, so this section is laid out in a slightly different way from the others, there being much smaller sub-sections as we work through each item briefly in turn.

Snap To Grid – Alt-D-S or Ctrl+Y

You can set CD! up so it has a visible or an invisible grid on the work page to help you position things accurately (see the next sub-section). With this setting enabled, CD! will ensure that when you move or re-size an object, the rectangular box which contains the object will align itself with the nearest grid line (depending on what type of change you are making).

Grid Setup... – Alt-D-I

The three dots at the end of this option tell you that it leads on to a dialog box which gives you control over a number of things.

- The measurement system used for the grid and the rulers

- The origin of the grid and the rulers (their 'zero point')

- The frequency (the 'mesh' size) of the grid.

The Display menu (Alt-D)

You can also determine whether the grid should show on screen or not. If you elect to show the grid, the work screen will acquire a rash of very fine, evenly spaced, dots.

Snap To Guidelines – Alt-D-G

This is similar to the previous option in that CD! will position an object to a particular alignment. The main difference is that you specify the alignment by setting up one or more guidelines. To demonstrate this we shall have to jump forward for a moment to the next but one setting on the menu, **Show Rulers**. If you already have rulers on screen, skip this next action paragraph.

1 Open up the menu and select the **Show Rulers** option (or tap Alt-D-R).

Once you have your rulers on screen you can set up guidelines dynamically, like this:

2 Move the screen pointer up and onto the horizontal ruler at the top of the screen. **CLICK AND HOLD** and then move the pointer downwards.

As you get back to the work area you will see the pointer dragging a blue dashed horizontal guideline with it.

3 Position the guideline somewhere near the centre of the page, then **RELEASE** the click.

232

The Display menu (Alt-D)

4 Now move to the left (vertical) ruler and repeat the process to position a vertical guideline near the middle of the page.

You can have as many as 50 guidelines set up if you want them (but we imagine you wouldn't then be able to see the wood for the trees!).

5 Now tap **Alt-D-G** (or 'open up the menu, etc.') to select the **Snap To Guidelines** option.

We can now try a couple of things to see the effects of switching this setting on.

1 Select the **Rectangle drawing tool** and position the crosshair pointer in the lower right quadrant of your marked up page. Place the cursor so it is near, but not touching, the two guidelines. Now draw a rectangle and watch what happens.

If you were within a certain distance of the guidelines you will have seen the rectangle snap its top and left sides to the guidelines, even though your screen pointer was not touching them. Now try this:

2 Select the **Pick tool**, then start to move the rectangle slowly downwards and to the right.

You will see the rectangle snap to and from the guidelines as you move. Try moving gently to and fro to see the snap in action.

The **D**isplay menu (Alt-D)

So guidelines are very useful for aligning things while you are creating a drawing. By the way, they won't print and they don't show when you get a preview. Even so, there will come a time when they get in the way. It is just as easy to get rid of guidelines as it is to set them up dynamically.

1 With the **Pick tool** still selected, **CLICK AND HOLD** on the vertical guideline and drag it off one side (either side) of the work area, then **RELEASE** the click. The guideline disappears. Use the same method to get rid of the horizontal guideline.

Guidelines Setup... – Alt-D-L

This option provides you with a dialog box which enables you to set up the guidelines by numbers rather than dynamically as you have just done. If you need absolute precision, then use this option instead of the dynamic method.

We don't really want to add anything more to that statement.

Show Rulers – Alt-D-R

If you have been working with this text, your rulers will already be on screen (if not, tap Alt-D-R or 'open up... etc.'). The measurement system and the zero point of the rulers will have been determined by the measurement system and the origin settings in force for the grid – either CD!'s default settings, or settings you have specified. CD! defaults to putting the origin, or zero point, at the bottom left hand corner of the page. We prefer to have the zero point for the rulers at the top left hand corner, so how do we change it quickly?

The Display menu (Alt-D)

1 Move the screen pointer to the top left hand corner of the screen, where the horizontal and vertical rulers intersect. **CLICK AND HOLD** and then slowly drag the pointer toward the top left hand corner of the work page.

When you get back onto the work area you will see that you are dragging two blue dashed guidelines.

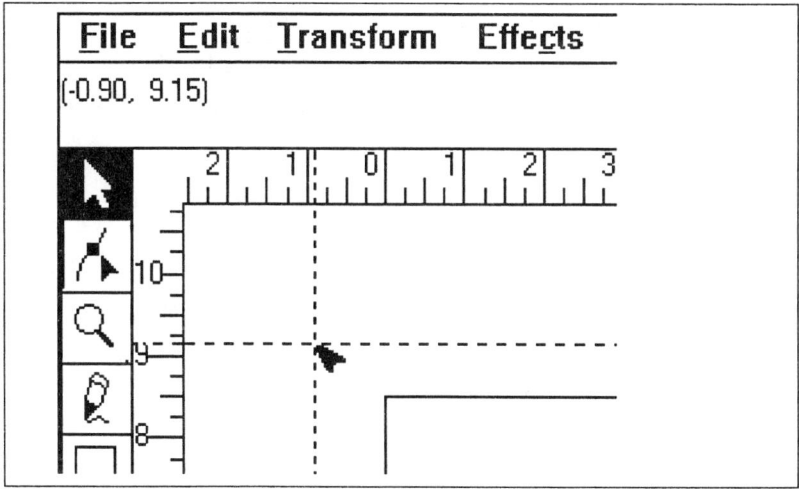

Fig. 5-12 **Setting the ruler zero points dynamically.**

2 Position the two intersecting blue dashed guidelines exactly on the top left hand corner of the work page and then **RELEASE** the click. (CD! will reset the zero points of the ruler (as well as the grid origin) to the position where the blue dashed guidelines intersected when you released the click.)

The Display menu (Alt-D)

Show Status Line – Alt-D-H

The Status Line is that part of the screen we have been calling the 'status area' – the area below the menu bar and above the start of the work area. This option enables you to 'toggle' the display of this area on and off. If you want more room on the screen, toggle it off, but if you want to keep track of what you are doing, leave it toggled on.

Show Colour Palette – Alt-D-C

Much the same comments apply to this option as did to the last. If you find it useful to have the colour palette at the bottom of the screen, leave it there. If not, toggle it off to give yourself more room.

Show Preview – Alt-D-P or SHIFT+F9

This option toggles the split screen preview on and off. We know that some people prefer to work with this preview switched on, but for us it slows things down too much – that is just our preference. You may prefer to work with it switched on. If you do, then you need to be aware that you do not have to accept CD!'s default setting. You can alter the sizes and positioning of the two screens. For example, if you grab the top edge of the preview screen and drag it down to a point where it is less than half its former height, you will get an 'over-under' split rather than a side-by-side split. If you then drag the left hand side of the preview screen to less than half its width, you will return to the side-by-side split. You can also increase or decrease the relative sizes of the work and preview screens by dragging on the left hand edge, in the side-by-side display, and the top edge, in the over-under display.

Experiment with these settings to see what you prefer.

The Display menu (Alt-D)

Show Full Screen Preview – Alt-D-F or F9 (or right mouse button)
This is the option we have been using from near the start of this book, so we do not have anything at all to say about it ... except, this is the option we prefer for everyday work with CD!. Oh, and this is particularly true when the right mouse button is set up to generate the display (via the Preferences options in the Special menu). Now we have nothing at all to say!

Show Preview Toolbox – Alt-D-T
You can have a toolbox for the preview screen as well as for the work screen. The preview toolbox, as you can see from this next illustration, is quite small, but it nevertheless has its uses. You can see that switching this option on gives you access to scroll controls and three icons. The top one works just like the zoom icon on the work screen. The bottom one gives you an over-under preview, the middle one gives you a side-by-side preview.

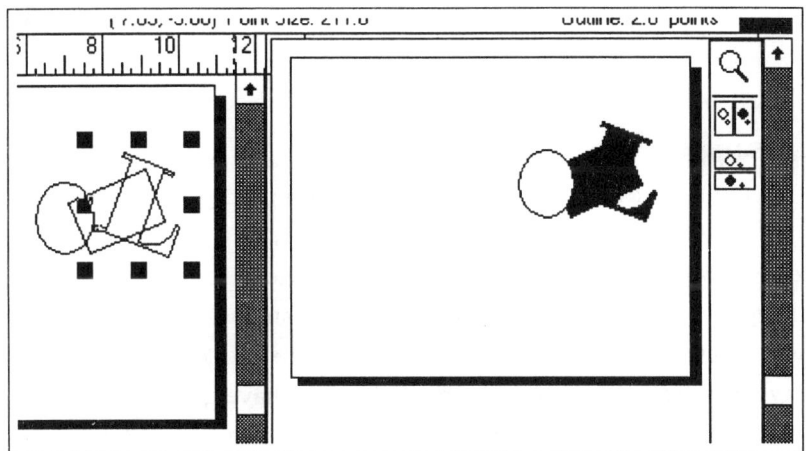

Fig. 5-13 **The preview toolbox selected (see the right hand side).**

The Display menu (Alt-D)

Preview Selected Only – Alt-D-O

When you are making adjustments to a small part of a complex image in the split screen display, you can speed things up by previewing only the object that you are adjusting. You can see the effect in the following illustration, where only the letter 'L' is selected.

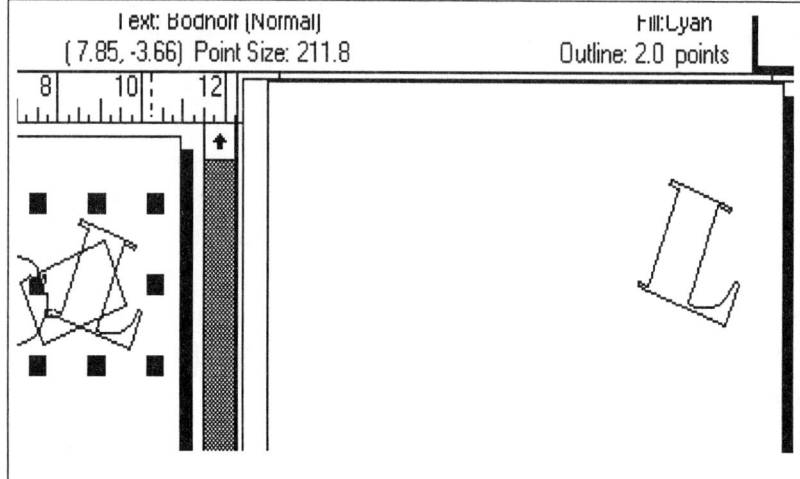

Fig. 5-14 **Preview selected item only.**

Auto-Update – Alt-D-A

This option provides another way of speeding up your work when you are working with the split screen display. When you toggle this feature off, CD! does not redraw the preview screen after every change you make to the image. So, you can make several minor adjustments to the 'wire frame' image on the work screen without having to wait between each one. When you have got things as you want them, you simply click on the preview screen and CD! will then redraw the updated image.

The Display menu (Alt-D)

Show Bitmaps – Alt-D-B

Yet another way to save drawing time is to switch the display of bitmaps off. CD! will show just the rectangle outline of the bitmap and not the detail of the bitmap itself (though it will be drawn on the preview screen). There are a couple of reasons why you might want to do this. Firstly, if you are editing a bitmap which you have traced, the editing process will be easier to carry out if the bitmap does not show. And following on from this, if you want to zoom-in to edit a fine detail, and the bitmap is still displayed, then the drawing time will increase the more you zoom-in.

Refresh Wire Screen – Alt-D-W or Ctrl+W

Occasionally, when you have been working quickly you might interrupt CD! while it is redrawing and you end up with blank patches on the wire frame image. This option refreshes the image so you can carry on working.

This, in our experience, is quite a rare event – it has happened only once since we started writing this book, but it still throws you when it happens. You begin to wonder how you managed to delete half a rectangle, or why a circle has a huge chunk missing. Ctrl+W puts it right immediately.

The Special Menu (Alt-S)

Bearing in mind that Step By Step books concentrate on those activities you will use most frequently when you are working with a particular piece of hardware or software, we have tended not to dwell on some of the more obscure aspects of CD!. As it happens, we have not omitted very much detail so far, but this menu is one which you will want to use only rarely (indeed, apart from the settings in the Preferences option, which we have used in earlier sections of the book and the quick way to create special arrowheads, you may never use the options in this menu at all), so we shall not spend much time discussing them. For the most part we shall limit our comments to summarising what they do.

Extract... and Merge Back... – Alt-S-X and Alt-S-M respectively
These two options exist so you can:

- extract text from your image in ASCII format – in other words in a form which can be edited in your word processor ... and when you have made your changes

- merge the text back in to the image.

If you find you need to use the procedures, see the CD! User's Manual, page 266.

Create Pattern... – Alt-S-C
If you think back to the sections about bitmap fills and vector fills you will remember that CD! has libraries of such pattern tiles. This option enables you to add to those libraries by copying an image or a part of an image and adding that copy to the range of fill patterns available.

The Special Menu (Alt-S)

Create Arrow – Alt-S-A

Begin by drawing an object of your fancy, as we did in the illustration below. We next 'Combined' the various objects into one and got the result you can see on the preview screen on the right.

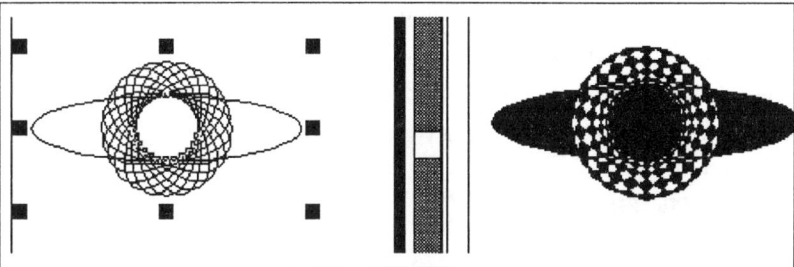

Next we selected this option by tapping in, Alt-S-A. CD! double checked that we knew what we were doing, but we reassured it and it went away to create an arrowhead with our fancy object. As you can see from this screen dump of the arrowhead library.

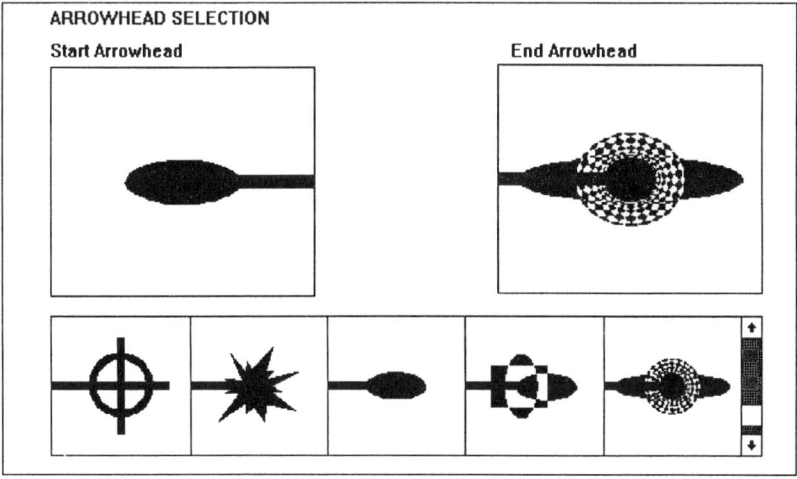

The whole process is very easy and very quick. Here you can see some of the results of our efforts. Impressive stuff, huh!?

The Special Menu (Alt-S)

Preferences... – Alt-S-E or Ctrl+J

As you have already seen, this option lets you set up CD! in accordance with certain preferred settings. When you select this option it leads on to a dialog box which in turn leads on to a further three, so you can state your preferences for a number of things. See page 275 of your User's Manual for a detailed description of the technicalities involved for each preference setting. And, once again, experiment to discover what is right for you.

```
PREFERENCES
  Place Duplicate:

    Horizontal: [ 0.25 ] [⬆⬇] [ inches          ]
      Vertical: [ 0.25 ] [⬆⬇] [ inches          ]


         Nudge: [ 0.10 ] [⬆⬇] [ inches          ]

    ☐ Cross Hair Cursor        ☐ Interruptible display
    ☐ Show Page Border         ☐ Use Mosaic

    [ Lines & Curves... ]  [ Print & Preview... ]  [ Mouse... ]

                              [   OK   ]   [ Cancel ]
```

Fig. 5-15 **The Preferences dialog box.**

The File Menu (Alt-F)
Starting and closing down

We cannot know precisely how your computer system is set up, because there are so many possibilities. For example, when you switch on in the morning, you might be faced with nothing more than an unhelpful 'System Prompt' (see the Glossary), or you may be faced with an applications menu, or the computer may go straight into running Windows 3, or even straight into running CD!. You may have to key-in a password to 'log-on' to a system. All of these are possible, indeed, fairly normal variations on a basic theme. So when we talk about starting up CD!, the best thing we can do is tell you what has to happen on any computer system and leave you to work out what is happening on yours.

We saw in an earlier section, that when you switch on your computer, it is effectively brain dead. It has to load an 'Operating System' – a program which manages its own operation – before it can function as a computer system. This gets the computer ready for work, but before you can load and run CD! you have to create the right environment for it by loading and running Windows 3. So the sequence of operations goes something like this:

1   **Switch on** the computer and wait for it to 'boot-up' (load its operating system). When you get the system prompt – **C:>** or similar... Key-in: **WINDOWS\WIN** and tap **RETURN** to get Windows running. (This assumes that your copy of the Windows 3 program is called WIN.EXE and it is stored in the \WINDOWS directory on the C: drive.)

The File Menu (Alt-F)
Starting and closing down

After a while you will get the Windows Start-up screen, which may or may not have the Program Manager Window on view.

2 Make the **Windows Applications** window active, then **DOUBLE CLICK** on the CD! icon to get CD! running.

As we said just now, there could be all sorts of variations on this basic procedure, it may even be fully automated, so CD! starts up 'by itself' when you switch the computer on (as it does on our system), but the automatic procedure 'batch file' still has to go through these essential steps.

3 When you get the CD! work screen, open up the **File menu.**

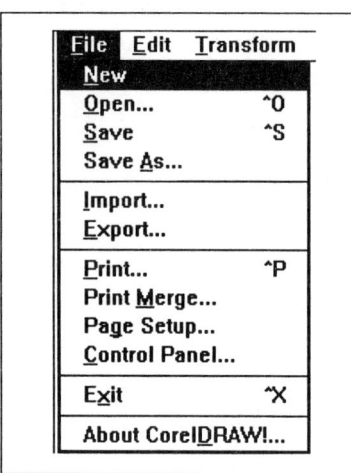

Fig. 5-16 **The File menu.**

If you want to create a brand new drawing, then you simply start creating. You do not have to open up the menu and select the **New** option. You use this option when you want to finish with the work you have on screen and start a new task from scratch. If you have made changes to the drawing on screen, since the last time you saved your work, CD! will ask if you want to save those changes before clearing the screen.

The File Menu (Alt-F)
Starting and closing down

You use the last but one item on this menu, Exit, when you want to finish working with CD!. You should always use this option (Ctrl+X, or Alt-F-X, or open up the menu and select the option) to close down. It ensures that CD! tidies up all its files and temporary files in an orderly manner. If you simply switch off without going through the proper close down procedure you might end up with all sorts of clutter on your hard disc.

Here also, if you have made any changes to the work page since the last time you saved, CD! checks to see if you want to save the changes. You have three options: 'Yes' do save, 'No' don't save, or 'Cancel' the exit command.

Like all good software, CD! won't let you do potentially destructive things to your work without checking. For all it knows, you might not realise that you have to save your work. Well, you don't <u>have</u> to, but there seems little point in doing the work if it's not worth keeping. You really ought to get into the habit of saving your masterpieces regularly and frequently – every 15 minutes or so. In fact, this goes for any work you do on a computer. If you live in the country like we do, and you have a power cut, it seems, every time the wind gets above force 5, then saving becomes a reflex action. It is amazing how much wasted effort this reflex avoids.

The first time you save a piece of work CD! doesn't know what to call your work, or where to put it on the disc. So, it displays the dialog box you can see on the next page. You use this dialog box to give it the details it needs.

The File Menu (Alt-F)
Saving your work

Let us assume, then, that you have been working on a drawing and the wind is getting up outside. You notice this and it reminds you that you haven't yet safeguarded your creative output.

1 For our purposes, just draw a rectangle, so we have something on the page.

2 Call up the **Save** option by, either tapping **Ctrl+S**, or tapping **Alt-F-S**, or by opening up the menu and selecting the third option down. The drawing is still untitled, so...

After a moment or two, the Save As dialog box appears on screen. Yours will not look exactly the same as the one from our system.

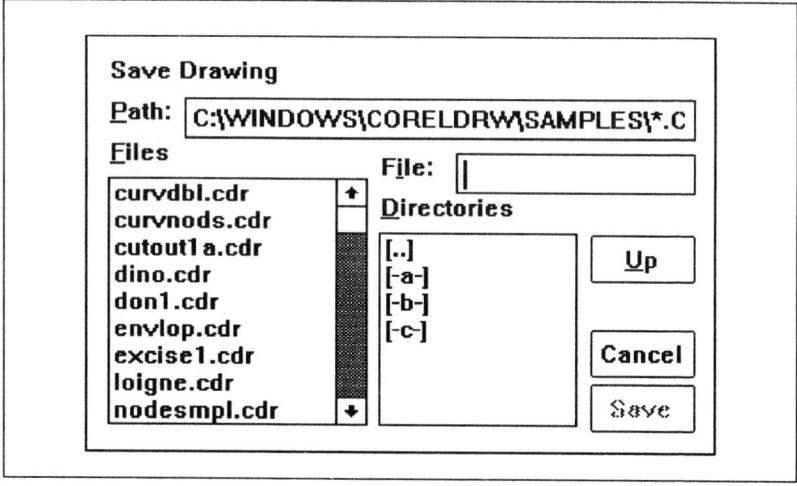

Fig. 5-17 **The Save As option dialog box.**

The File Menu (Alt-F)
Saving your work

There may be some terms on this dialog box which you have not encountered before, e.g. Path, or Directories. These are the names of DOS concepts – remember, even though CD! is running in the Windows 3 environment, MSDOS is the ultimate environment for the software on your system. When a Windows application wants to save or load files, it has to access the discs and it does this via DOS (MSDOS is short for 'Microsoft Disk Operating System').

The long box at the top of this dialog box shows the 'Path' which will lead to the file you are about to create. Interpreting it from the right, it tells you that you will be creating a file called something .CDR (on the illustration you cannot see the 'DR' of CDR, because it has been pushed off screen to the right, because the full path name is too long to fit into the box). The file, something-or-other .CDR (a file in CD! format) will be put into a directory, \SAMPLES, which is in the \CORELDRW directory, which in turn, is in the \WINDOWS directory on drive C:. The squarish box on the left of the dialog box is showing a list of the files called something-or-other.CDR which are already in the C:\WINDOWS\CORELDRW\SAMPLES path. The other squarish box is showing a list of the available drives on the computer system. The box labelled File: contains a straight line cursor. Although the illustration does not show it, this cursor is flashing as CD! waits for you to key-in an appropriate name for the file which will hold your work.

The File Menu (Alt-F)
Saving your work

You do not have to accept the path settings. So, let us be awkward and reject them and thereby put the file somewhere else on the hard disc. (If your hard disc is not called C:, then you will need to interpret the following actions to make them work on your system.)

1   **CLICK** on the button labelled **Up**. You will see the path name shorten by one directory name. The same thing happens as you: **DOUBLE CLICK** on the two dots **[..]** in the directories box.

These actions move you one step up the directory tree – i.e. closer to the 'root' directory of the hard disc, in which all the other directories on your system sit. (The DOS terminology is sloppy here, in that you don't move upwards to a root on a real tree, well not in England, anyway.) If you want to move further away from the root you click on the appropriate directory name in the directories box.

If you want to go direct to another drive, say, drive B: in our case, put a disc in the B: drive and then, to 'log-on' to drive B like this:

2   **DOUBLE CLICK** on **[-b-]** in the directories box.

For some reason, on our system, Windows takes four or five seconds to respond to the command, but eventually all the settings change.

3   Log back to drive C: then repeat either of the actions in paragraph 1 above until the path name reads **C:*.CDR**.

The File Menu (Alt-F)
Saving your work

So, we have told CD! that we want to save our file in the root directory on drive C:. Now we have to tell CD! the name we want to give to the file. DOS imposes certain rules which govern the names you can give to your files. File names can have two parts. The first not more than eight characters long for the name of the file, then a fullstop separating off an optional three letter 'extension' to the name that gives an idea of the type of file it is. You can use all the letters and most of the symbols on the keyboard, but we recommend you stick to using letters; they are easier to interpret.

For our purposes now, we can use a name which has a first part which is no longer than eight characters, which has no spaces and which does not have a fullstop (except at the end of the name and CD! will put that in for you normally, but see below).

1   Move the screen pointer to the box labelled **File** and **CLICK** once to make sure the cursor is active.

We know that the file will be called 'something dot (fullstop) CDR' and all we have to do is specify what the 'something' should be; CD! will add the dot and the CDR to indicate that the file is in CD! format. (N.B. If you don't want the file name to end in 'dot CDR' you do not have to accept CD!'s default setting. You can key-in a fullstop and up to three characters of your own to describe the type of file you are creating.)

2   Key-in the eight letter name **RECTANGL** (in upper or lower case).

The File Menu (Alt-F)
Saving your work

Notice that as you key-in the first character of the name, the 'Save' button changes from grey to black to tell you it is now available. The normal editing keys, such the cursor controls, Delete and BACKSPACE, are functional when you are keying text into the dialog box.

3 CLICK on the **Save** button (or tap the RETURN key) to implement your command.

The dialog box disappears while CD! creates the new file on the disc and saves the drawing and the other setting which are in force (such as, guidelines, the grid, the paper size and orientation, etc.). After a short pause you get the screen pointer back, which means you can carry on working. So saving your work is quick and easy. It is even quicker for the second and subsequent times you save the file, because, if you look at the top of the screen, you will see your drawing now has a title. So:

4 Start by making a change to the drawing – move it or re-size it, or skew it. You need to do this because CD! will only save files which have changed in some way since the last time you saved.

5 Tap **Ctrl+S** (or Alt-F-S or open up the menu and select the option).

CD! saves your work immediately under the title at the top of the screen. In other words, it updates the existing file and overwrites the version that was there before.

The File Menu (Alt-F)
Saving your work

Quite often, when you are developing and extending a basic graphic, you will want to save the current version without overwriting the original idea. The way to do this is to open up the original file (more of that in a moment), make the adjustments and then save the file under a different name, via the **Save As...** option from this menu. CD! will display the dialog box you have already seen and used, so we shall not bore you by repeating the exercise.

When you save files with the Save or Save As... options CD! creates or updates a file which is saved in its own .CDR format. Other software packages have different formats (e.g. we have already seen the difference between bitmap and vector graphics). Often you will create a drawing, using the flexibility and power of CD!, which you then want to use in, say, a publishing program like Ventura or Pagemaker. If that other software package cannot handle the .CDR format, then the only way to get the CD! drawing into it, is to save it (the drawing) in a format which the other software can read. You use the **Export...** option from the File menu to save a CD! drawing in a 'foreign' format.

Although the Export function is easy to carry out, there are a number of different variables to take into account. For this reason, we shall not go into the detail here. If you find you need to export a drawing from CD!, see your User's Manual, on page 173, which also refers you to the technical information in your Technical Reference booklet.

The File Menu (Alt-F)
Loading existing files

As you work with CD! you will build up your own library of images – always assuming you save all your work as we recommend. Quite often you will want to load one of those images, either to make changes or to print off a copy, or to export it. Here is how you do it.

1   Tap **Ctrl+O** (or Alt-F-O, or open up the menu and select the option). (If you have a drawing on screen and you have made changes to it since the last time you saved, CD! will ask you whether you want to save those changes (yes or no), or cancel the operation.) Choose **No** for this exercise, unless you particularly want to save the work.

CD! displays the dialog box you can see on the next page.

In the illustration we have clicked once on a file called 'DON1.CDR'. You can see on the left that the file name is highlighted and on the right you can see a square preview box which gives us a rough idea of what is in the file. The small black and white image allows us to tell quickly if it is the graphic we are looking for; the one we want to load. Assuming it is not the one we want, we can either, preview another file in the same directory (by clicking on its name), or we can move to another directory, just as we did when we examined the save procedure a short while ago, and preview the files in that directory.

Once we have found the file we want, we simply CLICK on the 'Open' button to load the file.

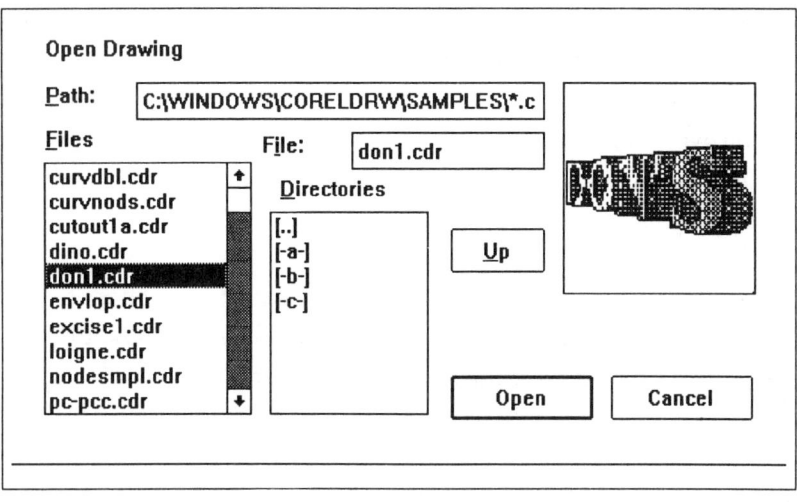

Fig. 5-18 **Opening an existing CD! file.**

In the same way that you can export images from CD! to other software packages, you can also import images from other software. Here too there is a wide range of possible variations, so we shall not go into detail. If you need to import an image, (e.g. from Windows Paintbrush), see page 170 of your User's Manual, which also refers you to the Technical Reference booklet. To see just how many possibilities there are:

1 Tap **Alt-F-I** (or open up the menu, etc.) and scroll through the options. (N.B. The option 'For Tracing' allows you to warn CD! that you will need a high resolution version of a bitmap to make the tracing function more accurate. But see page 172 of your User's Manual for the implications of using the option.)

The File Menu (Alt-F)
Printing your work

It seems to us that the whole reason for using CD! is to get pretty pictures onto paper. So the print process is very important. As far as CD! is concerned, getting a printout is very easy, but, before the print option will work, you must have installed the printer correctly via Windows 3 and you must have specified a default printer with the correct 'printer driver' (see the Glossary).

Installing the printer is very much a Windows operation and is outside the scope of this book, so if you do not know how to do it, see your Windows 3 documentation or get hold of a copy of 'Step By Step Using Windows 3' by Arthur Tennick (ISBN 0 7506 0080 2).

CD! will not print a blank page, so start by getting something, anything, on the work page. Then:

1   Tap **Ctrl+P** (or Alt-F-P, or open up the menu and select **Print**).

You will be offered the range of options you can see in the illustration on the next page. (See your User's Manual, starting on page 177 to find out what they all mean.) Here you can see we are using a Postscript printer which opens up a number of options which may not be available on your system.

2   For now, just **CLICK** on **OK** to get a printed 'hard-copy' of whatever is on your work page.

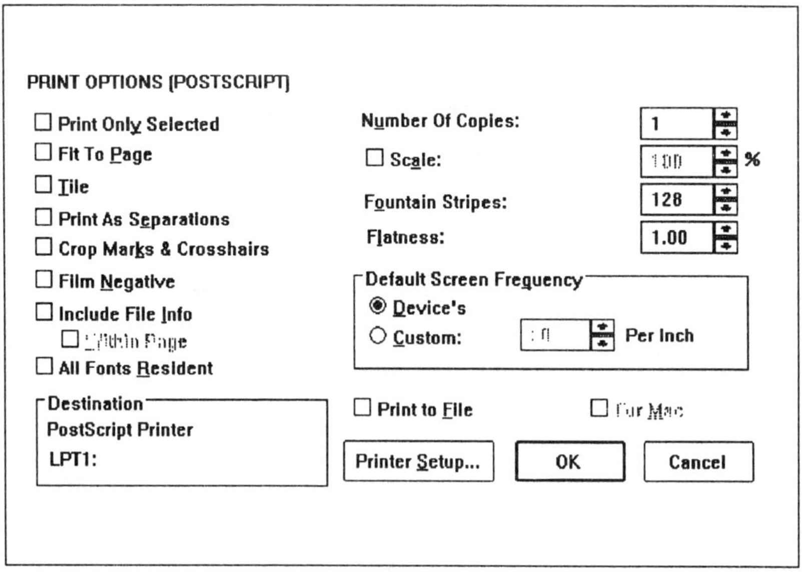

The File Menu (Alt-F)
Printing your work

PRINT OPTIONS [POSTSCRIPT]

☐ Print Only Selected
☐ Fit To Page
☐ Tile
☐ Print As Separations
☐ Crop Marks & Crosshairs
☐ Film Negative
☐ Include File Info
  ☐ Within Page
☐ All Fonts Resident

┌ Destination ──────
│ PostScript Printer
│ LPT1:

Number Of Copies: [1]
☐ Scale: [100] %
Fountain Stripes: [128]
Flatness: [1.00]

┌ Default Screen Frequency ──────
│ ⦿ Device's
│ ○ Custom: [0] Per Inch

☐ Print to File   ☐ For Mac

[Printer Setup...]   [OK]   [Cancel]

Fig. 5-19 **The Print dialog box.**

Simple drawings print fairly quickly, but allowing that CD! can create very complex images which include fancy fills as well as text, it is very easy to create files which take a very long time to print. Sometimes the only real answer is patience.

The file menu has another intriguing print option, **Print Merge...** In essence this option works just like the 'mailmerge' or merge print feature of a word processor. It is designed to enable you to create many copies of the same graphic file, but with different text elements for each one, which sounds interesting, but we wonder how often the typical user will want to implement it? If you do, see page 188 of the User's Manual.

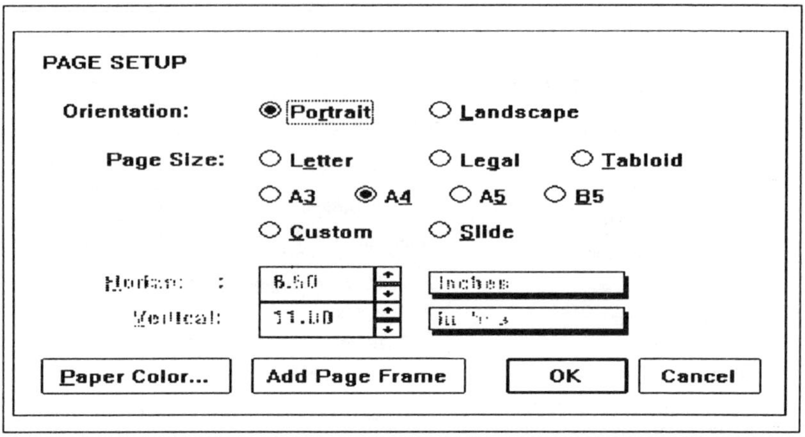

The File Menu (Alt-F)
Miscellaneous options

```
┌─────────────────────────────────────────────────────────────┐
│  PAGE SETUP                                                   │
│                                                              │
│    Orientation:     ◉ Portrait        ○ Landscape           │
│                                                              │
│      Page Size:     ○ Letter      ○ Legal    ○ Tabloid      │
│                     ○ A3   ◉ A4   ○ A5    ○ B5             │
│                     ○ Custom      ○ Slide                    │
│                                                              │
│    Horizon:  :   │ 8.50  │▲▼│   │ Inches    │               │
│    Vertical:     │ 11.00 │▲▼│   │ in...     │               │
│                                                              │
│   │ Paper Color... │   │ Add Page Frame │   │ OK │  │ Cancel │ │
└─────────────────────────────────────────────────────────────┘
```

Fig. 5-20 **The Page Setup dialog box.**

You can call up this dialog box in the usual ways – Alt-F-G, open up the menu and select the option – or you can DOUBLE CLICK on the outline of the work page, with the Pick tool selected. We doubt if the purpose or the contents of this dialog box need much explanation but if you want to be absolutely certain, see page 191 of your User's Manual.

Control Panel: The 'control panel' which you access via this option is actually the Windows control panel. This enables you to check or make adjustments to the various Windows system settings. As you will be working in Windows when you use this option, check your Windows documentation to see how it works.

About CorelDRAW!... displays information about your software system, and it tells you how much disc space you have left.

256

PART SIX
Quick Reference

A few last words

Our whole aim in writing this book has been to get you off to a flying start; that's what Step By Step books are for. It has meant that we have not indulged in rambling discussions of underlying theory, but rather we have tried to describe how and why you do certain things to get results with CD!. We have provided the essential theory, as and when it was relevant, but, for example, we would have liked to include a lot more information about Windows 3 and about DOS. Had we done so, this would have been a much larger and more expensive book – it would not have been a Step By Step book at all!

Yet to get the best from CD!, or any other software package, it really does help to have a good grasp of what actually happens when you implement a certain command. It is analogous to driving a car; you don't <u>have</u> to know how the engine works, or what happens when you depress the clutch pedal, but, if you do know, then it puts you in greater control of the machine. So find out as much as you can, perhaps by getting other Step By Step books on the background topics.

As we said right at the start of the book, we are very impressed with the power and flexibility of CD! and now we hope that some of our enthusiasm has trickled through to you. It is also worth repeating what we have said at various points in the book; experiment with the various tools CD! offers you! Develop your own ways of doing things, design your own effects, because, after all is said and done, CorelDRAW! is nothing more than a set of tools for you to use. To help you use them more efficiently, we shall finish off the main part of the book by listing all the keyboard shortcuts, in the following quick reference pages. Have fun..!

Quick Reference:
The F keys

F1	none set for this key

Select ZOOMS

F2	Zoom-in one step
F3	Zoom-out one step
F4	Fit image in window (show all of the image)
SHIFT+F4	Show page (all of work page)

Select DRAWING TOOLS

F5	Line & Curve tool
F6	Rectangle tool
F7	Ellipse tool
F8	Text tool

Selecting PREVIEWS

F9	Full page (also via the right mouse button, if set-up via the Preferences dialog box)
SHIFT F9	Split screen

Selecting ADJUSTMENT TOOLS

F10	Shaping tool
F11	Fountain fill
SHIFT F11	Uniform colour fill
F12	Outline PEN settings
SHIFT F12	Outline COLOUR settings

Quick Reference: Menu shortcuts

FILE Menu

Ctrl+O	**Open** an existing CD! file
Ctrl+S	**Save** the file you are working on
Ctrl+P	**Print** the file you are working on
Ctrl+X	**eXit** from CD!

EDIT Menu

Alt+BACKSPACE	**Undo** (cancel) the latest action
Alt+RETURN	**Redo** the cancelled action
Ctrl+R	**Repeat** the previous action
SHIFT+DEL	**Cut** (delete) the selected object(s), putting a copy on the Windows clipboard
Ctrl+Insert	**Copy** the selected object(s), putting a copy on the Windows Clipboard
SHIFT+Insert	**Paste** an item from the Windows Clipboard into the file on screen
Delete	**Erase** or **Clear** object(s)
Ctrl+D	**Duplicate** the selected object(s)
Ctrl+T	**Edit** existing text

TRANSFORM Menu

Ctrl+L	**Move** object(s)
Ctrl+N	**Rotate & Skew** object(s)
Ctrl+Q	**Stretch & Mirror** object(s)

Quick Reference: Menu shortcuts

EFFECTS Menu

Ctrl+B	**Blend** between two objects
Ctrl+E	**Extrude** the selected object

ARRANGE Menu

SHIFT+PGUP	Move object **to top** (or front) of stack
SHIFT+PGDN	Move object **to bottom** (or back) of stack
PGUP	Move object **one place forward** (or up) in stack
PGDN	Move object **one place back** (or down) in stack
Ctrl+G	**Group** two or more objects
Ctrl+U	**Ungroup** grouped objects
Ctrl+C	**Combine** two or more objects into one
Ctrl+K	**Break** a combined object **apart**
Ctrl+V	**Convert** an object **to curves**
Ctrl+A	**Align** objects or text objects
Ctrl+F	**Fit text** to a specific **path**
Ctrl+Z	**Align** (text) **to baseline**

DISPLAY Menu

Ctrl+Y	**Snap to grid** on/off
SHIFT+F9	**Split screen preview**
F9 (or RIGHT mouse button)	**Full screen preview**
Ctrl+W	**Refresh wire screen**

SPECIAL Menu

Ctrl+J	**Set preferences** for CD! operation.

Quick Reference: Associated Corel Programs

The CorelDRAW! version 2.01 package comes complete with three associated 'utility' programs, i.e. programs which are designed to enhance CD!'s operation. They are: CorelTRACE!, Mosaic and WFN BOSS.

- CorelTRACE! enables you to trace bitmap images from a scanner or another art package and convert them into CD!'s vector image format. Once in this format they can be processed like any other CD! image and this generally means that you can get a much higher quality output when you come to print the image with CD!.

- Mosaic is primarily intended to be a visual file selector. It provides you with a visual display of the contents of files created with version 2.0 or later of CD!. You can use Mosaic, either as a stand-alone program in its own right, or you can set it up to work from within CD! (via CD!'s Preferences dialog box).

- WFN BOSS has two main functions: it enables you to create CD! typefaces by converting fonts from other font suppliers and secondly it enables you to create your own symbols and fonts in the WFN format, and so use them directly in CD!.

Each of these products has its own User Guide, so if you need more details on what they can do for you, consult the relevant booklet.

If you are using CD! to provide artwork for a desk-top publishing system, make sure you have a look at the technical reference handbook as well, it contains lots of useful tips and hints.

Quick Reference:
Where do we go from here?

If you are just embarking on your work with CD!, you have a fascinating journey ahead of you. If you would like to swap stories with other travellers, you might like to join the CorelDRAW! Users Club. Contact them at:

CDR (The Logical Extension to CorelDRAW!)
10 Highfields Road
Mountsorrel
Loughborough
LEICS LE12 7HH

Glossary
Appendix

Glossary

In the main body of the book we have tried to define jargon words as they arose. This appendix takes that process a little further by gathering together a few more definitions for some of the jargon surrounding computers in general.

ALT Key
A key which works like a 'super' shift key. It enables the keyboard to generate ALTernative results using the various keys on the keyboard.

Ambiguous (file names)
With DOS you can key in commands which include file names incorporating 'wild-card' characters - i.e. characters which represent another character (see 'Wild Cards') - thus creating a file name ('mask') which can apply to more than one file. In this sense such file names are ambiguous.

Artwork
Finished graphics and text ready for the 'page-make-up' or duplication stages of the print process.

ASCII
A standard computer industry code for representing letters, numbers, symbols etc. - American Standard Code for Information Interchange.

Ascender
That part of a lower case letter which ascends above the normal letter height (example, the letter 'h' has an ascender).

Glossary

Aspect Ratio
The relative proportions (length of sides to width of top and bottom) of a piece of artwork.

Back-up
(verb) The process of creating duplicate copies of files or discs.
(noun) A duplicate - safety copy of a file or disc.

Baseline
A theoretical line on which the letters in a typeface stand.

Bleed
The space on a page between the text area and the edges of the page.

Body Copy
All text on a page other than headings, sub-heads, captions, etc..

Body Type
The typeface used for body copy.

Booting
The start-up procedure for a computer system, during which the computer 'reads-in' the operating system from disc.

Bullet
A large dot or other symbol used to highlight and mark the beginning of an item in a list.

Glossary

Camera Ready
Completed artwork which is ready for the next (photographic) stage of the print production process.

Command
An instruction (or a set of instructions) keyed in at the keyboard, telling the computer to carry out a particular job.

COM
The file name extension used for a 'command file' - a computer program written in the computer's internal language.

Copy
(verb) To make a duplicate version of a file or a disc.
(noun) An impressive way of saying 'text'.

Copyfitting
The process of making text fit into the space available for it.

Cropping
Trimming a photograph or an illustration to get just the bit you want. You might then have to 'scale' it to fit into the space available for it.

Cursor
A marker on your screen, usually a bar or rectangle of light. It is there to tell you where you are working on the screen display.

Glossary

Cursor Keys

A set of keys marked with arrows pointing up, down, left and right. You use these keys to move the cursor around the screen.

Data Disc

A disc on which you store files you have created by using a computer program.

Data File

A file which holds information, as opposed to a file which holds a program.

Default Settings

When you start up a computer system or a software program it has to make certain assumptions about the way you want to work. It has to adopt standard settings for a wide range of things. Thus the program will work in a particular way in 'default' of any instructions to the contrary. In other words it will adopt certain 'default settings'.

Delete or Erase

To rub out or erase items which have put themselves in by mistake.

Descender

The bit of a lower case letter which hangs down below the baseline (as in 'g' or 'j' or 'p').

Disc (or Disk)

A flat circular piece of plastic with a magnetic surface which you use to store 'permanent' copies of data and program files.

Disc (or Disk) continued

A 'Floppy Disc' has a semi-rigid plastic sleeve which has slots to enable the computer to read the information stored on the disc.

Disc Drive

The part of the computer system which spins the disc while the computer is reading from or writing to it.

Documentation

The manuals supplied with your PC or its software, which are supposed to explain how to use the system.

Dot Matrix Printer

A printer which uses a set of pins to create a pattern of dots on paper. By varying the pattern you create the shapes of the different characters.

DPI

Short for 'Dots Per Inch'. When you produce finished output (with anything other than a daisywheel printer), the quality of that output is measured in DPI. The higher the number of DPI the better the quality of the output.

Dropped Cap(ital)

Large capital letters are sometimes used for the first letter of a paragraph. Such letters are called 'dropped' caps when the first letter drops down from the top of text instead of standing up above the rest.

Glossary

Editing
The process of amending, inserting or deleting text and layouts which someone else has fouled up.

Em
Technically, an Em is the square of the size of the typeface - so a 36 point Em will measure 36pt by 36pt. In practice, when designers or printers talk about Ems they usually mean a 12pt Em (i.e. a space measuring 12pt by 12pt, or 1/6th of an inch square, or yet again, 1 pica square).

En
A space which is half as wide as an Em.

ENTER Key
The key with which you 'enter' (i.e. confirm) your instructions or selections from menus. The RETURN key performs the same function in most kinds of software, though it can vary.

File
A collection of information stored as a separate entity with its own special filename. You can have data files and program files (i.e. files which hold programs).

File Name Mask
See 'Ambiguous'.

Floppy Disc
A flexible sheet of recording material in the shape of a disc.

Glossary

Font (Fount)

A complete set of type of one style and size (source, OCD).

Format

(noun) 1. The layout of a page.

(noun) 2. The method for organising the storage space on a disc.

(verb) To prepare a disc for use on your computer system by laying down a new pattern of magnetic 'tracks' on its surface ready to store information.

Function Keys

A set of keys on your computer keyboard which are pre-programmed to do certain jobs (i.e. to perform certain functions).

Galley

The end result of the typesetting process - a long strip of typeset text ready to be cut and pasted-up.

Gutter

The white space between adjoining columns of text.

Half-tone

A photograph is made up of continuous shades or tones, but the print process cannot reproduce these, so printers break up the initial image into a pattern of dots - the different intensities simulating a continuous gradation of tones. (See also 'Screening'.)

Glossary

Hard Copy

A copy of your work printed out on paper. Also known as a 'printout'.

Hardware

The physical components which make up your computer system, such as the keyboard, disc drive, monitor, printer.

Housekeeping

Those necessary activities which are not concerned directly with using your computer for applications, but without which, things would soon get in a mess. For example, carrying out routine checks of what information you are holding on a particular disc, erasing unwanted material, renaming files, copying files, etc..

Hyphenation

Fitting lines of text into the space available for it by breaking some words into two and distributing the two sections of the word between the end of one line and the start of the next. The first part of the word (and therefore the line) ends in a hyphen.

Input

(verb) The process of getting information into a computer system.
(noun) Information which has been put in to a computer system.

Justification

The process of lining text up to a margin (also known as 'ranging' the text). The text in this glossary is 'ranged right' as well as 'ranged left'. Text can also be ranged to the centre of the space available.

Glossary

'k' or 'K'

This is short for kilo, or one thousand bytes. Actually there are 1024 bytes in one kilobyte, so in computer terminology '1k' actually means 'near enough a thousand'.

Kerning

The process of adjusting the space between letters.

Laser Printer

At first glance it looks like a photocopier and, indeed, it works in a very similar way, except, the image is created in the computer rather than by a photographic process.

Layout

The plan for how the final page will look.

Leading

(Pronounced 'ledding') is the space between lines of typeset text - it used to refer to the strips of lead which were used physically to separate lines.

Ligature

Certain groups of letters which look better when 'run together' as a single character (e.g. ffi, ll).

Measure

Printers' term for the width of the line (in picas).

Glossary

Memory The computer's 'internal store' in which it holds programs and data while you are working with them.

Menu
A list displayed by a computer program that tells you which activities are available at a particular point in the program.

Monitor
A high quality screen or 'visual display unit' (VDU) which enables you to see what you are keying in, as you key it in. It also displays the results of the computer's processing activity.

Mouse
A device which enables you to 'input' instructions to the computer by moving a pointer on your screen, (so it points at a picture or a menu), rather than by keying in lengthy sequences of commands.

Operating System
A type of computer program which controls or 'manages' the way the computer and all the other items of hardware operate as a single system.

Orphan
A single word moved onto a new column or page during copyfitting (small relative of a 'widow').

Output
(verb) To transmit information from the computer or some other device.

Output continued

(noun) The information you get out of your computer (via the printer, or a disc drive, or on screen).

Overmatter

Bits of text left over after copyfitting.

Overwrite

To write data on top of data which is already stored in the computer's memory, or on disc, and thus replace it.

Page Make-up

The actual process of assembling text, illustrations, headings etc. into the finished page.

Pica

A unit of measurement equal to about 1/6th of an inch.

Point

A unit of measurement equal to 1/12th of a pica - roughly 1/72nd of an inch. (To be very precise, 72 points = 0.996264 ins.)

Printer

(1) The machine attached to the computer which prints out hard copies of the work you have been doing.

(2) The person who says he will have the printed copies of your work ready on Thursday – just as he did last week.

Glossary

Printer Driver

That software which controls the printer.

Prompt

An instruction on the screen telling you what to do next.

Proportional

On a typewriter and on your computer's screen, an 'i' takes up the same amount of space as an 'm'. With proportional spacing, the different sizes of the letters are taken into account when the text is laid out, so an 'i' takes up about half the space of an 'm'.

Quit

To finish doing a particular job with your software, or finish working with the software itself.

Ragged Edge

Text which has only one end of its lines lined up vertically.

RAM

Random Access Memory. That part of the computer's memory which is available for you to use for loading and running programs and for entering and processing data.

Record

A single set of data held in a data file. A data 'file' contains a number of 'records', each one consisting of individual 'fields'.

Glossary

Reformat

(In word processing) to change the layout (i.e. the format) of text, giving it, for example, different margins, page lengths and so on.

Reset

To repeat the start-up or 'Boot' procedure.

Resolution

The number of dots per inch printed by the printer, or the number of elements (pixels) per inch which make up the image on the computer screen.

ROM

Read-Only Memory. The computer memory in which information is stored permanently and cannot be altered by program instructions.

Rule

Printers' jargon for a straight line.

Scale (or 're-scale')

Adjusting the size of an illustration to make it fit the space available.

Scanner

A device for converting images into a form which the computer can manipulate.

Screening

The process by which a photograph (with continuous tones) is converted into a pattern of dots (half tone).

Glossary

Scrolling

The process of moving your screen display (or part of it) up and down or side to side to enable you to get a particular section of the display on screen.

Software

Programs which enable the very stupid hardware to do a useful job.

Text

The words and characters (letters, numbers, spaces and symbols) which make up a finished document. In CD! you can have 'String' text, which you place directly on the page ... and 'Paragraph' text which you enclose in a bounding box on the page. The two types of text behave differently when you, for example, stretch and scale them.

Tint

A particular density of dots in an image. Different tints produce different shades of grey in a black and white reproduction process.

VDU

See Monitor.

Wild Cards

A character which can be used in file names to represent another character (just like wild cards in poker). In DOS there are two wild card characters '?' and '*'. The '?' represents any other single character, the '*' represents any group of characters.

Glossary

Widow

A single line of text which is pushed into the next column or onto the next page during copyfitting (a bigger version of an orphan).

Word Processor

A computer driven by a software program that enables you to carry out the tasks of writing, editing and printing all kinds of documents.

Word Wrap

A word processing feature in which the software works out where a line of text should end and it then 'wraps' any uncompleted word down to the left hand end of a new line, so you can keep typing without having to worry about when you get to the end of your typing line.

Wire Frame

The outlines which make up your CD! image.

WYSIWYG

'What You See Is What You Get'. A computer text and picture processing feature in which the screen display closely emulates how the finished document will look on the page.

Index

Index

Index

Index

Index

Index

Index

Addendum - CorelDRAW 3.0

Corel Corporation have just announced details of CorelDRAW 3.0. This is a major upgrade to the program which includes enhancements to CorelDRAW, CorelTRACE and Mosaic, plus three new programs - CorelCHART, CorelSHOW and CorelPHOTO-PAINT.

The new program set is being released on both floppy disk and CD-ROM - both in the same box. The cost of upgrading to the floppy version will be £99, the cost of the CD-ROM version will be £89. Considering that both are in the same box that's a little bit odd but that's the way it is. The new version should be available around the end of July 1992. The CD-ROM version contains over 14,000 Clip-Art images plus 2,500 symbol images. (That is not a misprint!)

By the end of the year the CorelDRAW Graphics Package will be available for Windows, OS/2, Unix and the Mac. It is available in English, Danish, Dutch, French, German, Italian, Spanish, and Swedish amongst others.

There are over 200 enhancements and improvements which means that there is insufficient room here to cover these in depth, but what follows is a list of the major new features.

CorelDRAW

The program no longer uses WFN fonts. Instead the package comes complete with 153 TrueType fonts. The CD-ROM contains an additional 100 TrueType fonts plus all 253 fonts in Adobe Type 1 format. The only things that remain in the WFN format are the Symbol Libraries. However, you may still use the old fonts if you wish.

Addendum

CorelDRAW now allows you edit directly on the colour preview screen. You have a choice of using either the wire frame or the preview mode - and can switch between the two as necessary.

The program runs about three times faster - even in full colour mode - but its performance is even more dependent on your system resources.

The package is the first major software release to be fully Windows 3.1 compatible. CorelDRAW itself can act both as an OLE Client and Server.

Text is now entered directly on screen, though the dialogue box is still available, and can be edited and manipulated there.

CorelDRAW allows an unlimited number of layers, the only limiting factor is your system resources. Each layer can be locked, coloured, visible and printed individually and separately. Layer names are user defined.

The program now provides full context sensitive help at every level. F1 gives you the full help and Shift-F1 gives you the context sensitivity.

Roll-up dialogue boxes have been included. These are a new innovation, invented by Corel, which allow you to have certain dialogue boxes on screen all the time but they roll up like window blinds until they are needed.

Menus have been changed slightly so that their contents are more logical.

CorelDRAW 3.0

Dialogue boxes have been changed to conform to the Windows 3.1 standard and they are all now 3-D.

At the bottom of the File menu, a Drawings List is now included that contains the path and filenames of the last four files opened so you can reopen one quickly and easily.

Printing is much faster and you have far greater control over various settings.

On-screen colours in the Preferences dialogue box have been simplified: you either use dithered colours or pure colours depending on your monitor and graphics card.

A new Snap to Object command has been added which allows you to align objects very precisely.

With the Layer you can now define any object as a grid so that you are no longer limited to just horizontal and vertical lines. You can have circles, diagonal lines, freehand lines, text, whatever you wish as a grid.

The program now includes a comprehensive Spell Checker and Thesaurus.

The importation and exportation of images has been greatly enhanced, although you still cannot re-import an EPS file that has been exported. You can now import any of the following: AI, BMP, CGM, DXF, EPS, GEM, GIF, HPGL, PCX, PIC, PICT, PIF, TGA, TIF, WMF. You can export any of these formats: AI, BMP, CGM, DXF, EPS, GEM, GIF, HPGL, PCX, PFB, PICT, PIF, SCODL, TGA, TIF, TTF, WMF, WPG.

Addendum

There are major enhancements to the Blend feature. You can now blend interactively on-screen, have a blend follow a path, select alternative colours and the whole thing is now dynamic. Change the starting or ending object, either by moving it or resizing it, and the blend redraws automatically. You can blend group as well as individual objects. You can also blend a number of objects to the same path.

The major enhancements to Extrude include interactively. You now longer have to worry about x,y coordinates because you can now do it directly on screen. Once the extrusion has been drawn you can assign any colours to it, set the light source position so that the extrusion has defined shadows. You can even rotate the whole thing in three dimensions!

Fit Text to Path has been greatly improved. Text can now be fitted interactively, changed, realigned, moved and otherwise enhanced. You now have a choice of 60 possible combinations of ways to align the text - all of it interactively. Because the path is now dynamic you now have total control over changing things. Move the path and the text automatically moves to refit itself.

The Perspective feature has been improved to make it friendlier and easier to use.

The application of fills has been dramatically improved. You can now change the way a fountain fill appears directly on screen, via the fill roll-up, without having to mess around with dialogue boxes. Bitmap fills can now be tiled directly on screen.

CorelDRAW 3.0

CorelTRACE

There are few changes to this. Basically the program has been speeded up, and there is better control of its options. Batch conversion is now much better.

MOSAIC

Mosaic can now see just about every graphics file format you care to mention - and display them all in full colour. The formats available are: AI, BMP, CCH, CDR, DIB, EPS, GIF, PCC, PCX, SHW, SHB, TIF and TGA.

You can print directly from Mosaic and define how the images will be printed. Use this to make your own catalogue of clip-art. And you can print all the file formats.

Mosaic can search and sort files on the basis of name or keyword, which you assign when you save a file.

Create and expand CorelDRAW library files, though using the CD-ROM makes this unnecessary.

CorelCHART

This is an entirely new program and it is a full feature data-charting package. (A bit like Excel gone graphic.) The program allows you to generate charts from data quickly and easily. The program can act as an OLE client.

3D charts can be rotated, zoomed, panned, switched, etc. with ease.

Addendum

Data can be imported directly from Excel, Lotus 123, Harvard Graphics, dBase and others.

The chart types available include: Dual Axes, Bipolar, Stacked, Side by Side, 100% Graph, Logarithmic scales, 3D, Pictograph, Pie charts, Ring charts, Scatter graphs, Spectral graphs, Histograms, Tables and Clustered graphs. Horizontal bar, line and area. Types can be combined for dramatic effect.

Pictographs can be imported from just about any graphics package you care to name and in full colour.

You have total control over the axes, scale, grid, titles, sub-titles, legend and footnotes. All can be moved, resized, defined and manipulated at will.

Pie slices can be moved, exploded and deleted interactively on screen.

CorelPHOTO-PAINT

This is the second new program is the set. (Actually it is ZSoft's PhotoFinish which Corel have licensed in its entirety.) It is a bitmap manipulation and enhancement program, probably the best one on the market today.

The program includes a vast range of tools including polygons, colour replacer, eyedropper, blend, smudge and smear, gradient, lasso and magic wand.

Photo-Paint includes brightness and contrast control, colour to grey-scale mapping and equalisation controls. It includes features which allow you to remove spots, sharpen and blend images. You can also emboss, motion blur, edge detect and mosaic any part of an image.

The program gives you total control over colours, and/or grey-scales, with image conversion, colour similarity, colour balance and tolerance. It is 25-bit colour compatible which means you can have 16.4 million colours.

You can import PCX, TIF, GIF, BMP, TGA, MSP and export files in any of these formats plus EPS.

Variable zoom allows you to use all the tools at any magnification.

CorelSHOW

This is the third new program and it allows you to do powerful and dynamic on-screen presentations.

The program is Windows 3.1 compatible and acts as an OLE client and all that implies.

On the CD-ROM there are over 100 predefined backgrounds.

Slide show features include over 20 transition effects including time delay, explode, blind and others.

Elements of any slide can be highlighted during a presentation. The program also allows you to include full animation within a slide show. The CD-ROM includes over 100 flicks for you to use.

PC PLUS STEP by STEP

This series, designed for clarity and ease of use, is intended for those who wish to get off to a flying start when faced with new software, operating systems or machines. These books take you through, step-by-step, the processes and functions that will enable you to maximise your effectiveness FAST. The books are written by users for users and are now published in association with PC PLUS, the UK's best-selling PC-specific magazine. The Step by Step series and PC PLUS magazine provide the complete package for all IBM - Compatible personal computer users.

WORDPROCESSORS

Using Locoscript PC (Version 1.5)
John Campbell
0 7506 0249 X   £14.95

Using MS Word 5.0
Roger Carter
0 434 90316 7   £14.95

Using Word for Windows
Alan Balfe
0 7506 0205 8   £14.95

Using Wordperfect for Windows
Arthur Tennick
0 7506 0359 3   £14.95

Using Wordperfect 5.0
Gautier
0 434 90656 5   £14.95

Using Wordstar 5, 5.5 & 6
Alan Balfe
0 7506 0341 0   £14.95

SPREADSHEETS

Using Excel 3.0
Roger Carter
0 7506 0360 7   £14.95

Using Lotus 1-2-3 Macros
Ian Sinclair
0 7506 0198 1   £16.95

Lotus 1-2-3 for Windows
Arthur Tennick
0 7506 0607 X   £14.95

Using Lotus 1-2-3 Release 3
Stephen Morris
0 434 91292 1   £14.95

Quattro Pro 3
P K McBride
0 7506 0358 5   £14.95

DATABASES

Paradox 3.5 for Windows
P K McBride
0 7506 0610 X   £14.95

Using Q & A
Roger Carter
0 4349 0224 1   £14.95

Using Superbase 2 & 4
Arthur Tennick
0 7506 0042 X   £14.95

Using dBASE IV
Roger Carter
0 434 90251 9   £14.95

Utilities

Using Disk & RAM Utilities
Ian Sinclair
0 434 91892 X   £14.95

Operating Systems

MS—Dos 5.0
Alan Balfe
0 7506 0471 9   £14.95

CP/M Plus on the Amstrad PCW
John Cambell
0 7506 0460 3   £14.95

Using Windows 3
Arthur Tennick
0 7506 0080 2   £14.95

Machine Guides

Exploiting the Amstrad PCW 9512
John Campbell & Marion Pye
0 7506 0075 6   £14.95

Using the Amstrad PCW9512
John Campbell
0 7506 0169 8   £12.95

Using the Amstrad PC1512/1640
Second edition
Morris
0 434 91266 2   £14.95

Desktop Publishing

Ventura 4.0 for Windows
John Campbell
0 7506 0632 0   £14.95

Corel Draw 2.0
John Cambell & Marion Pye
0 7506 0503 0   £14.95

Pagemaker 4.0 for Windows
Alan Balfe
0 7506 0634 7   £14.95

Programming

Using Quick Basic 4.5
Stephen Morris
0 7506 0220 1   £14.95

Programming in G-W Basic
P K McBride
0 7506 0256 2   £14.95

Visual Basic
Stephen Morris
0 7506 0633 9   £14.95

Also of Interest

A series of handy, inexpensive, **pocket size reference books** to be kept by the computer and used every day. Their size makes them an ideal 'travelling' companion as well. **All titles are hardback.**

Newnes MS-DOS Pocket Book 2nd Edition
Second edition
Ian Sinclair

Over 110,000 copies sold of the 1st edition This best-selling title has been enlarged and updated to include material on version 5.0.

0 7506 0328 3   £9.95

Newnes MAC Users Pocket Book
Steve Heath

A handy all-round reference book for users of any MAC machine.

0 7506 0083 7   £12.95

Newnes PC Printers Pocket Book
Stephen Morris

Will be invaluable to anyone who has a program that requires them to set up their own printer codes, anyone having a problem with their printer or wants to use some of its more exotic facilities.

0 7506 0197 3   £12.95

Newnes C Pocket Book
Conor Sexton

Covers in as succinct a manner as possible the C language as defined by the ANSI standard.

07506 0221 X   £12.95

Newnes Data Communications Pocket Book
Second edition
Michael Tooley

Will be invaluble for anyone involved with the interconnection of computer systems: from technicians and engineers to managers involved in the purchase of datacomms equipment.

0 7506 0427 1   £10.95

Newnes PC Users Pocket Book
Jim Reid

Based on the IBM PC range, including 286, 386 and 486 models. Will appeal to all programmers and computer enthusiasts.

0 7506 0085 3   £12.95

Newnes Hard Disk Pocket Book 2nd Edition
Mike Allen & Tim Kay

A comprehensive guide to hard disk, covering every aspect from the disk manufacture, the drives and their components, organization, utilities and data safety.

0 7506 0470 0   £12.95

Newnes 8086 Family Pocket Book
Ian Sinclair

A portable guide to the Intel family of 16/32 bit processors. Covers the 8086, 8088, 80186, 80188, 80286, 80386 and 80486 types.

0 434 91872 5   £10.95

Newnes Windows 3 Pocket Book
Ian Sinclair

Features the use of Windows 3 with MS-DOS 5, a combination which will be increasingly common as users change over to version 5.0

0 7506 0347 X   £12.95

Newnes Unix Pocket Book
Heath

There are many UNIX books around but none that contain all the information necessary to get the best out of the system - This book does just that.

0 7506 0391 7   £12.95

Newnes Computer Engineers Pocket Book
Third edition
Michael Tooley

An invaluble compendium of facts, circuits and data that makes an indispensible guide to the designer, service engineer and all those interested in computer and microsystems.

0 7506 0372 0   £12.95

Related Titles...

The Chaos Cookbook
Joe Pritchard

Examines chaos theory in a much more practical way than other books and includes type-in-and-go listings which even the initiated will appreciate.

0 7506 0304 6 £16.95

Designing your systems with Smartware II
Martin Gandolf & Michael Hicks

Introduces the concepts and principles of system design and shows what must be considered when developing your own system using Smartware II. Essential for all users of the popular and powerful integrated package.

0 7506 0425 5 £19.95

Wordstar Professional Handbook Version 4
John Campbell

Provides a source of basic information while leaning and then as a handbook of practical tips and memory joggers once you have mastered the essentials

0 434 90242 X £22.50

Using Pagemaker 3.0 on the IBM-compatible AT
Alan Balfe
Complete with appendices covering associated programs, this guide will allow you to realise and master the power and potential of PageMaker 3.0

0 434 91318 9 £16.95

Using Ventura 2.0
John Campbell

Contents: Making a Start; The basic tools; What you do - and how; Fine tuning - getting the details right. John Campbell is an experienced trainer and hasthe knack of covering the ground in the right sequence so that one piece of information leads naturally to another.

0 434 90272 1 £16.95

Lotus Symphony 2.0 Handbook
Stephen Morris

The aim of this book is to show you how to get the most out of Symphony 2. The emphasis is on practical applications, with examples drawn from many different aspects of business.

0 434 91302 2 £17.50

Using SuperCalc 5.0 in Business Spreadsheets in 3 dimensions
P K McBride
INCLUDES FREE DISK

Explores and explains the huge potential of the system with the 3d capabilities very much in mind. The free disk contains copies of the sheets used in the book and blank sheets ready to be tailored to your needs.

0 434 91308 1 £27.50

Hypertalk and Hypertext Programming the Interface graphic in the Macintosh and Windows 3 with Hypercard 2 Plus
A E Stanley

Presents the fundamental working of GUI in the context of object-orientated programming tools for the end user. All command/ functions and uses of Hypertalk and Hypertext are covered.

0 7506 0500 6 £19.95

Wordcraft 6 Handbook
Sue Horrocks

Contents: System requirement; Operating system; Installing WordCraft; WordCarft basicsl Modes of operation; Menus; Basic text controls and commands; Using text; Designing and editing a report using advanced features; Spell check; Printing; Using images in text; Troubleshooting.

0 434 91324 3 £30.00

Macintosh Business Book
Joe Sudwarts

Written by an internationally known expert, this book covers everything from initial hardware and software selections to the effective use of networking, information exchange and communication for the Mac User in business and coporation environment.

0 7506 0502 2 £21.95

Scanning and Printing Perfect Pictures with Desktop Publishing
Peter & Anton Kammermeier

Provides all DTP users who want to integrate photos in their documents with practical hints and numerical values for image editing and printing. Aimed at the beginner as well as the professional user.

0 7506 0539 1   £36.99

Servicing Personal Computers
Third Edition
Michael Tooley

The revised and enlarged version of this bestselling book contains a new chapter on servicing 68000-based microcomputers. It has also been updated throughout and contains many new photographs and diagrams.

0 7506 0374 7   £25.00

The Scanner Handbook
A complete guide to the use and applications of desktop scanners
Stephen Beale & James Cavuoto

An authoritative and informative guide to selecting, installing and using a desktop scanner. Offers practical tips and indispensable advice throughout.

0 434 90069 9   £19.95

Wordperfect for Windows:
A Guide to Professional Document Production
Andrew Glynn Smail

Considers how to achieve predetermined goals in document production, rather than merely acquainting the reader with the use of the functions of the program.

0 7506 0541 3   £19.95

ORDER FORM

Title	ISBN	Price	Qty	Total
	UK & Surface Postage & packing			£2.00
		Grand Total		

❏ **Please send Airmail (extra costs will be charged)**
❏ **Cheques/Postal Order enclosed**
   (Cheques should be made payable to Butterworth-Heinemann Ltd)

❏ **Credit Card**   ❏ **Access**   ❏ **American Express**   ❏ **Visa**   ❏ **Diners**

❏❏❏❏❏❏❏❏❏❏❏❏❏❏❏❏   **Expiry date** _ _ _ _ _ _ _ _ _ _ _ _ _ _ _ _ _ _ _

Name _   **Company** _ _ _ _ _ _ _ _ _ _ _ _ _ _ _ _ _ _ _

* Address _

_ _

Tel No _ _ _ _ _ _ _ _ _ _ _   **Signature** _ _ _ _ _ _ _ _ _ _ _ _ _ _ _ _ _ _ _   **Date** _ _ _ _ _ _ _ _ _ _ _

* If paying by credit card use address shown on your credit card statement.

Please return this form to:
Alice Scott-Taylor, Butterworth-Heinemann Ltd, Linacre House, Jordan Hill, Oxford OX2 8DP.
Alternatively, phone our distribution centre direct on 0933-410511, quoting ref: B2900
(Please have credit card details ready) **PRICES ARE SUBJECT TO CHANGE**

FUTURE PUBLISHING - HOME OF BRITAIN'S BEST-
SELLING COMPUTER MAGAZINES - DEDICATED TO
BRINGING YOU THE LATEST NEWS, PRACTICAL
ADVICE, UNBIASED REVIEWS AND PURCHASING
GUIDANCE TO ENSURE YOU GET THE VERY BEST OUT
OF YOUR PC AND YOUR SOFTWARE.

PC PLUS - the complete package for all PC users

Over 420 pages packed with:- the latest news and independent reviews of the major
hardware and software releases; 'HelpScreen' offering handy tips and practical
advice; 'Programming Workshop' enabling you to program easily and effectively; the
'PC Buyers Guide' with over 1,000 listings so you can locate products, services and
suppliers and, for your protection and peace of mind, there is our exclusive Buyers'
Protection Scheme.

Our policy is to inform, explain, and help - rather than blind you with jargon and baffle
you with acronyms. With PC PLUS, you not only get unbiased purchasing advice, you
also get a whole host of features that help you to get more from your PC, improve
your effectiveness, and save time and money.

On top of all this vital information, you also get a cover-mounted disk with every single
issue. You can choose to receive your personal copy with either a 3.5" or 5.25" disk
but, whatever the format, every disk is packed with tools, programs and useful utilities
which will help you to get even more out of your equipment and software.

You gain all these benefits when you subscribe

• Your copy is guaranteed - avoid the disappointment of missing an issue.

• Your copy is delivered to your door at no extra charge - save yourself the time and
hassle of having to go and find your copy every month.

• You protect yourself against inflation - the price you pay now is held for the duration
of your subscription. Even if the cover price goes up, you don't pay a single penny
more.

• You get first refusal on all special mail order offers we run - normally at money-
saving prices exclusive to subscribers.

• You have a cast-iron guarantee. You can cancel your subscription at any
time in the future and will refund you for all unmailed issues - no quibbles, no risk.

PLEASE ENTER MY SUBSCRIPTION FOR 12 ISSUES OF PC PLUS AT THE MONEY-SAVING PRICE TICKED BELOW

❏ UK **£29.99**　　❏ Europe **£74.19**　　❏ Rest of World **£123.59**

PLEASE TICK THE FORMAT OF DISK THAT YOU REQUIRE

❏ **5.25"**　　　❏ **3.5"**

TO ENSURE THAT YOUR MAGAZINE AND DISK ARRIVE QUICKLY AND UNDAMAGED, ALL OVERSEAS SUBSCRIPTIONS ARE SENT AIRMAIL. THESE COSTS ARE INCLUDED IN THE ABOVE PRICES.

Name _____ Tel No _____

Address _____

_____

_____ Post Code _____

METHOD OF PAYMENT

❏ Access/Visa　CARD NO ❏❏❏❏ ❏❏❏❏ ❏❏❏❏ ❏❏❏❏

　　　　　　　EXPIRY DATE ❏❏❏❏

❏ Cheque　　MAKE CHEQUES PAYABLE TO FUTURE PUBLISHING LTD AND SEND WITH THIS CARD IN AN ENVELOPE TO THE FOLLOWING ADDRESS:

PC PLUS subscriptions, Freepost, The Old Barn, Somerton, Somerset TA11 7BR

Signature _____ Date _____

This subscription coupon valid only until 31 Dec 1992　　　　BHFP001